# Decorate

## Cakes, Cupcakes, and Cookies

# WITH KIDS

**Creative Publishing
international**

First published in the United States of America by
Creative Publishing international, Inc., a member of
Quayside Publishing Group
400 First Avenue North
Suite 400
Minneapolis, MN 55401
1-800-328-3895
www.creativepub.com

Visit www.Craftside.Typepad.com for a behind-the-scenes peek at our crafty world.

ISBN: 978-1-58923-776-6

Digital edition published in 2014
eISBN: 978-1-61058-874-4

10 9 8 7 6 5 4 3 2 1

Library of Congress Cataloging-in-Publication Data Available


Copy Editor: Catherine Broberg
Proofreader: Karen Ruth
Book Design and Page Layout: *tabula rasa* graphic design (www.trgraphicdesign.com)
Photographs: Dan Brand

Printed in China

# Decorate
## Cakes, Cupcakes, and Cookies
# WITH KIDS

Techniques, Projects, and Party Plans
for Teaching Kids, Teens, and Tots

Autumn Carpenter

**Creative Publishing**
**international**

# Contents

# Introduction

SPENDING TIME BAKING in the kitchen with a child not only creates lasting memories but also teaches children a rewarding life-long hobby. Piping buttercream icing or working with rolled fondant feels like playing and is a creative (and delicious!) way for children to express themselves. Decorating also gives children a wonderful sense of accomplishment, no matter how young the child. Making treats with kids for a party can save money and will impress their friends. Homemade treats created by children make excellent gifts for friends, teachers, or loved ones. Invite your child's friend to spend the day baking and decorating. It's a great way for children to spend a few hours with a friend. Surprise your child and transform an ordinary day into an extra-special day by working together to create a beautiful, delicious dessert for dinner. Whether you want to spend an hour or a full day in the kitchen, this book offers plenty of projects to choose from.

## A CLEAN AND SAFE KITCHEN

Before getting started working with children in the kitchen, take some time to teach smart kitchen skills. Here are the basics that every child should know.

- Ask an adult for help when using electrical appliances, such as a mixer.
- Have an adult remove baked goods from the oven.
- Check the expiration date of the food items you are using. Make sure the dates have not passed.
- Wash your hands with soap and water before you begin to bake or decorate and after every time you lick your fingers!
- If trimming a cake with a cake slicer or knife, ask an adult for help.
- Cleanup is part of the baking and decorating process! Wipe up any spills to avoid slipping and falling in the kitchen.
- Read all the instructions *before* beginning and gather everything you need before starting the projects.

## HOW TO USE THIS BOOK

Baking and Decorating Basics covers the ABCs of working in the kitchen, such as baking cakes, cookies, and cupcakes. After the baking basics, learn how to pipe with buttercream or cover cakes and treats with rolled fondant. Finally, find out how to make chocolate candy treats to coordinate with the cake or cupcakes—recipes include suckers, dipped pretzels, dipped cookies, and cake balls.

Party Themes covers decorated projects for fifteen different themes, seasons, and holidays. Whether you copy the ideas from this section exactly or use the techniques shown to decorate your own theme, you can create cakes and treats that are sure to impress! The projects feature clear instructions with step-by-step images. Most of the projects and techniques can be created with minimal adult help for children 10 and older. Each project is graded for difficulty with one to three stars: one-star projects are easy; three-star projects are more complicated and may be best suited for older children. Suggestions are given on ways to include younger children no matter how difficult the project.

Writing this book was so much fun—especially when it meant spending time with my four children, my friends and their children, my sister, mom, nieces, nephews, and in-laws. Several of the adults and children who helped me were new to decorating, but once they got started were inspired to try their own projects. I hope you enjoy the book and use it to create memories with the special little ones in your own life.

# Baking & Decorating Basics

This section begins with a supply list for baking and decorating. After the tools, learn the essentials of baking cakes, cupcakes, and cookies. Next, learn how to ice cakes and treats with buttercream. Using pastry bags and piping fundamentals with the most popular piping tips are shown in this section. Simple instructions are given for covering cakes, cookies, and cupcakes with rolled fondant. Finally, instructions are included to make coordinating treats such as chocolate suckers or cake balls.

# Baking Tools

### COOLING RACKS
It is important to cool cakes, cookies, and cupcakes on a cooling rack (1) to avoid the bottoms from becoming soggy. Choose a cooling rack with a close wired grid to prevent small cookies from slipping. Stackable cooling racks save space.

### JUMBO SPATULA
A spatula (2) with an extra large blade (usually 10" to 12" [25.4 to 30.5 cm]) is useful when lifting cakes.

### PASTRY BRUSH
A pastry brush (3) is used to apply pan grease to cake pans.

### PAN GREASE
Pan grease (4) is a commercially made recipe for bakers that helps cakes release properly from pans. There is no need to flour the pan if pan grease is used.

### CAKE PANS
Cake pans (5) come in basic shapes, such as round, square, or rectangle (sheet cake pans), as well as shaped characters or themes. The amount of batter needed will vary according to the size of the pan (see the chart on pages 22 and 23). Aluminum pans are most common. Cake pans with a dark finish are likely to brown cakes quicker; reduce the temperature 25° when using dark pans. Pantastic pans are made of a plastic that withstands heat and must have a sheet pan underneath when baking.

### CAKE CARDBOARDS
Place baked and cooled cakes on the same size of cardboard (6) if placing the cake on a cake stand. Waxed cardboards are available to prevent oils from the cake and icing from soaking into the cardboard, causing the board to warp. Cakes that will not be on a decorative stand should be placed on cardboards or cake drums (thick foil-covered cardboards) larger than the cake.

### CAKE SLICERS
Slice domed cakes evenly with a cake slicer (7). Cake slicers can also be used to divide a cake for filling. A slicer with an adjustable blade allows for more possibilities.

*(continued)*

## CUPCAKE PANS

Three sizes of cupcake pans (1) are most popular: standard, mini, and jumbo. Heavy-duty aluminum pans work best. Cake batter should be baked as soon as possible after it is mixed, so for standard cupcakes it is good to have two pans, each with twelve cavities.

## ROLLING PINS

A rolling pin (2) is used to prepare cookie dough, rolled fondant, or gum paste. A baker's rolling pin doesn't have handles, which is ideal because it allows the weight to be distributed on the barrel and is less likely to cause fatigue in the hands and wrists. A silicone rolling pin won't stick to cookie dough. A classic, wooden rolling pin is always a nice choice. Some rolling pins come with rings that fit on each end of the barrel to aid in rolling the dough evenly (an alternative to perfection strips). Rings may also be purchased separately for rolling pins with certain diameters. Choose a rolling pin that is wide enough to handle a large sheet of cookie dough. The more the cookie dough is rolled, the more the dough becomes overworked. Children may have better control using a rolling pin with a small barrel, but the dough will need to be re-rolled several more times compared to a rolling pin with a longer barrel.

## PERFECTION STRIPS

Perfection strips (3) ensure uniform thickness when rolling out cookie dough or rolled fondant. The strips come in a set with several different thicknesses. Place the cookie dough between two strips and roll until the dough is the same thickness as the strips.

## COOKIE CUTTERS

Thousands of cookie cutter shapes (4) are available in nearly every theme imaginable and in a variety of finishes. The most popular finishes are copper, tinplate, plastic, plastic-coated metal, and stainless steel. Tinplate cutters are inexpensive and will bend easier than copper or stainless steel, but in most cases can be bent back to the original shape. Copper and stainless steel are more durable and will hold their shape after cutting dozens of cookies. Copper cutters are usually not as sharp as tinplate cutters. Take care when washing all metal cutters as they may rust or discolor if not thoroughly dried. Plastic cutters or plastic-coated metal cutters do not rust and are not as sharp as other cookie cutters, making them an obvious choice for children.

## CUPCAKE CORERS

Add yummy fillings using cupcake corers (5), available in a range of diameters. An apple corer also works well for coring cupcakes.

## COOKIE SCOOPS

Filling cupcake pans using a cookie scoop (6) keeps the pan free of messy batter and allows you to scoop equal amounts in the cavities. Use a 2-ounce scoop to fill standard cupcakes with a full, rounded top.

## SILICONE BAKING MATS

Silicone baking mats and parchment paper (7) are used on cookie sheets to keep cookies from sticking. Parchment paper comes on a roll or in convenient pre-cut sheets. The sheets can be reused several times in the same baking day. Silicone mats come in several sizes. Choose a mat that most closely fits on your cookie sheet to maximize the amount of space used. It is handy to have two or three mats to keep the baking process efficient.

## COOKIE SHEETS

Cookie sheets (8) come in a variety of finishes, styles, and sizes. Choose a shiny silver, generously sized cookie sheet that will allow at least 1" (2.5 cm) between the oven wall and cookie sheet for even heat circulation. A 14" × 20" (35.6 × 50.8 cm) cookie sheet fits in standard ovens. Choose one with no sides or one side to allow a spatula to easily slide under cookies near the edges of the sheet. Cookie sheets with a dark finish tend to brown the bottoms of the cookies too quickly. Do not grease cookie sheets unless the recipe calls for grease as this may cause cookie dough to spread. Keep two or three cookie sheets on hand for efficient baking. Allow sheets to cool between batches; placing dough on hot cookie sheets will cause the cookies to spread.

1

2

2

3

8

6

5

7

4

# Decorating Tools

## PASTA MACHINE
As an alternative to a rolling pin and perfection strips (page 12), a pasta machine (1) can be used to ensure that rolled fondant is rolled to an even thickness. Pasta machines or pasta machine attachments for standing mixers make it quick and practical to roll out small amounts of rolled fondant. Generally, flowers and accents should be rolled thin; use setting #4 or #5 on standard pasta machines. Before inserting rolled fondant into the pasta machine, knead and soften the fondant. Roll slightly thicker than the first setting. Set the pasta machine to the thickest setting (usually #1). Insert the fondant into the pasta machine. Crank the handle, or turn on the mixer if using the attachment. Take hold of the fondant as it is fed through the bottom of the machine. Turn the setting to the next thinner setting and feed the fondant through again. Continue feeding the fondant and turning the dial to a thinner setting between each roll.

## PASTRY ROLLER
A pastry roller (2) is a small rolling pin used to smooth crusted buttercream cakes.

## KNIFE
Use a paring knife (3) for cutting small pieces of rolled fondant.

## RULER
A stainless steel ruler (4) ensures that cut strips are straight.

## CLAY GUN/EXTRUDER
An extruder (5) is a tool that creates ropes with consistent thickness. The extruder kits contain a variety of interchangeable disks for making strands in different shapes and sizes.

## MINI PIZZA CUTTER
Trim off excess rolled fondant after the cake is covered with this handy tool. The mini pizza cutter (6) also works well for cutting strips to make a striped cake, or for making loops for a bow.

## FONDANT SMOOTHER
Fondant smoothers (7) ensure that your rolled fondant–covered cake is smooth and satiny. Glide over the cake with the smoothers to remove wrinkles. Smoothing the rolled fondant with your hands may leave unsightly indentations.

## CUTTERS
Use cookie cutters to cut out both the cookie and the rolled fondant. Cutie cupcake cutters (8) are small cutters designed to cut shapes of rolled fondant to place on cupcakes. Other metal cutters can be used to cut pieces for accents on cakes, cookies, and cupcakes. Strip cutters (9) are very useful for making stripes and are used on many projects throughout the book. Tiny cutters are handy to cut small designs for accents on cupcakes or cookies.

## PLUNGER CUTTERS
Plunger cutters (10) cut and remove the rolled fondant shape with the push of the trigger. The two-step action makes these plungers handy for quickly cutting flowers, leaves, snowflakes, and more. Some plungers will emboss details onto the cut rolled fondant.

## BRUSHES
Use brushes (11) with large, soft bristles to brush shimmery dusting powders on treats. Use small brushes for adding dots of piping gel as accents on cakes, cookies, and cupcakes. When covering cookies with rolled fondant, first brush piping gel on the baked cookie as an edible glue. Also, use a pastry brush to remove excess powdered sugar from the surface of rolled fondant–covered cakes and cookies.

## FOAM PADS AND BALL TOOL
A foam pad (12) is used to cup small flowers. Place the cut flower on the pad and use a ball tool to cup the petals.

## FLOUR SHAKER
Use a flower shaker (13) to sprinkle controlled amounts of powdered sugar onto the work surface. Choose a shaker with a fine mesh screen to ensure the work surface is not over dusted.

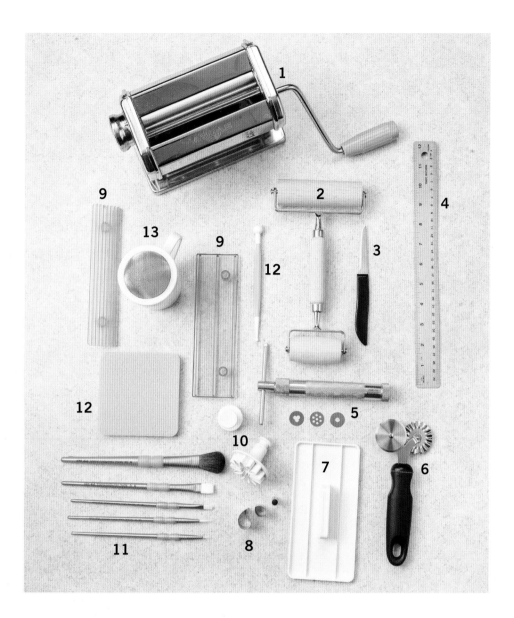

## SILICONE MATS AND PARCHMENT PAPER

Set dipped chocolate coated treats onto parchment paper to set. Prevent rolled fondant from sticking to the work surface by rolling it on silicone mats. Note: The mat will likely still need to be dusted with powdered sugar before rolling. (See page 12)

## ROLLING PINS

Rolling pins designed for rolled fondant work the best. Use a large, heavy rolling pin with a smooth finish to roll fondant. A wooden rolling pin may transfer a slight wood grain from the pin. A silicone rolling pin is wonderful for cookie dough but tends to pick up lint, which will end up on the rolled fondant. (See page 12)

*(continued)*

## CANDY MOLDS

Candy molds (1) are used to make accents for cakes or to create coordinating treats with chocolate coating. Candy molds are made using food-grade materials and are available in nearly any theme. Silicone molds give outstanding details with chocolate coating and rolled fondant. Sucker molds are popular to use for parties and gift giving.

## PASTRY BAGS

A variety of pastry bags (2) are available for piping. Reusable pastry bag are economical if decorating several cakes throughout the year. Choose a reusable pastry bag that is thin, lightweight, and conforms to your hand when squeezed. A 12" (30.5 cm) bag is standard for common use. The smaller the bag, the easier it is to control, though smaller bags will have to be filled more often. Disposable, clear bags are ideal to use with children so they can see the icing colors. Disposal bags also make cleanup a bit easier—especially helpful when working with children who tend to be a bit messy. Use pastry bag ties or twisties to keep icing from spilling out of the bag. Again, this is especially helpful when decorating with kids.

## DECORATING TIPS

Pipe a variety of shapes, sizes, and designs with decorating tips (3). The chapter on Piping Using Tips, page 40, covers the most popular tips and their uses. Tip-cleaning brushes, invaluable for cleanup, have a small cylindrical brush for scrubbing the inside of tips.

## COUPLER

A coupler (4) is a two-part tool used to interchange tips while using the same pastry bag. It also keeps the icing from seeping out of the bag. A coupler has two parts: a base and a screw.

## DIPPING TOOLS

Use dipping tools (5) designed for candy making to easily remove treats from melted chocolate candy coating.

## ICING SPATULAS

Small spatulas (6) are used for icing cupcakes and cookies. They are also used for lifting small rolled fondant accent pieces. Small, angled spatulas work well when crumb coating the cake with buttercream icing. Large spatulas are used for icing the cake. Choose a spatula with a thin blade that is as long as the cake's diameter.

## TURNTABLE

Placing the cake on a turntable (7) makes it much easier to spread icing on the side with consistent pressure.

## FLOWER FORMERS

Shape flowers or other cut pieces of rolled fondant, such as the cowboy hat brim (page 78), with flower formers (8). Allow the pieces to dry for several hours or over-night to retain their formed shape.

# Edible Decorating Supplies

## SPRINKLES AND SUGARS

Sprinkles and sugars add color, sparkle, and crunch. Sanding and coarse decorating sugars (1) are coarser and sparkle more than granulated sugar. Sprinkles and edible confetti (2), available in various shapes and colors, add instant decorations to simple iced cookies and cupcakes. Jimmies (3) are tiny cylinder-shaped candies. Use round candies for flower centers or polka dots. Nonpareils (4) are tiny decorative balls. Sugar pearls and candy beads (5) are larger than nonpareils. Sixlets (6) are small, pea-size candy-coated balls with chocolate on the inside. These candies are available in several colors.

## SUGAR LAY-ONS, CHOCOLATE ROCKS

Icing decorations (7) are made by piping royal icing onto parchment paper to create designs. Royal icing shapes can also be purchased. For example, several sizes of premade eyes are available. Molded sugar pieces (8) are also available in a variety of designs. Chocolate rocks (9) are delicious and add an instant realistic decoration to treats.

## DUSTING POWDERS

There are a few types of dusting powders (10). Some have a shimmer and are available in many metallic colors, including gold, silver, copper, and pearl. A silvery-white pearl is one of the most useful powders, as it can be brushed on any color to give a soft pearl metallic sheen. The powders can be brushed on dry in powder form for an all-over application. Brush dusting powder onto treats with a firm finish, such as rolled fondant or finished pieces of chocolate candy. If a metallic shimmer on a buttercream iced treat is desired, use a metallic food color spray. Dusting powders may be mixed with grain alcohol to create a paint. Some dusts are nontoxic, but not yet FDA approved, and are recommended for decorative purposes only.

## DISCO DUSTS

Disco dust (11), sometimes called fairy dust, provides the most sparkly effect; it is nontoxic but not yet FDA approved. Disco dust should be used on treats as decoration only and not for consumption. Remove any accent with disco dust from the cake or cupcake before serving.

## EDIBLE GLITTER

Edible glitters (12) are small edible flakes that give a subtle sparkle under light. Edible glitter is available in flakes or in an extra-fine powder, called edible glitter dust. These products do not add flavor or texture. Sprinkle onto icing while it is wet, or brush piping gel on the treat to adhere the glitter.

*(continued)*

## BUTTERCREAM

Buttercream (1) is a classic American icing that is fluffy, sweet, and can be spread or piped on cakes, cookies, and cupcakes. It is available commercially or can be made from a recipe.

## PIPING GEL

Piping gel (2), available in a tub or a squeeze tube, is a clear, flavorless gel that acts as edible glue for attaching edible decorations to cakes, cookies, and cupcakes. Decorations can be placed on the icing while the icing is wet, or piping gel may be used as a glue to attach the decorations. Piping gel is also brushed onto baked cookies before attaching rolled fondant. Piping gel can also be colored blue to resemble water.

## ROLLED FONDANT

Rolled fondant (3) is an icing used to cover cakes that provides a smooth, satiny finish. It can also be used for molding or cutting accents for cakes, cookies, and cupcakes. It is available commercially or can be made from scratch. Tip: Before trying out a recipe, buy commercial rolled fondant to become familiar with the texture.

## GUM PASTE

Though gum paste is made of all edible materials, it dries very hard so is used only for decorative purposes. Its elasticity allows it to be rolled nearly translucent for the most dainty accents. It can be made from scratch, purchased commercially, or made by adding food-grade tylose (4) to rolled fondant. Add approximately 1 tablespoon of tylose to 1 pound of rolled fondant.

## FOOD COLOR

Food color (5) is used to color cake batter, icings, chocolate candy coatings, rolled fondant, gum paste and more. Gels, pastes, and powdered colors are highly concentrated and are best suited for coloring. Liquid colors require a large amount of coloring to obtain vibrant colors and may affect the consistency of icings and rolled fondant. Powder color should be mixed with vegetable shortening to eliminate speckling if adding the color to buttercream icing or rolled fondant. If coloring chocolate or candy coating, use an oil-based food color. Powdered food color can also be used for chocolate or candy coating, but it may leaves tiny specks of color. Dissolve the powder in a small amount of liquid vegetable oil before blending.

## FOOD COLOR SPRAYS

Aerosol color sprays (6) provide instant colors to iced cakes, cupcakes, and cookies. They are available in popular colors as well as metallic sheens like pearl, gold, and silver.

## CHOCOLATE CANDY COATING

Chocolate coating (7)—sometimes called candy melts, compound coating, almond bark, or confectionary coating—is an easy-to-use melting chocolate for dipping and molding. Chocolate coating is available in milk chocolate, dark chocolate, white chocolate, and many colors. It is also available flavored and colored, such as peanut butter, mint, and butterscotch. The milk and dark chocolate coatings contain cocoa powder and oils. The white and colored coatings contain sugars and oils. Read the label before purchasing the candy coating. If the label lists cocoa butter as an ingredient, the chocolate must be tempered (a process not covered in this book) before dipping or molding; otherwise, the chocolate will not set up properly and may be spotty and chalky. Candy coating can be found in candy supply stores and in some grocery stores.

## CHOCOLATE TRANSFER SHEETS

Chocolate transfer sheets (8) are acetate plastic sheets with a design that adheres to warm chocolate or chocolate candy coating. When the chocolate candy coating is set, peel back the design, and the design remains on the hardened candy.

## FOOD COLOR MARKERS

Food color markers (9) are pens filled with food color. Use these to apply color on any edible icing or product that forms a crust, such as rolled fondant or edible frosting sheets. The markers do not work well on chocolate coatings, as the water-based food coloring repels the oil-based coatings.

## CANDY WRITERS

Candy writers (10) are tubes of chocolate candy coating. These tubes are used to paint details in molds or onto small treats. The candy coating inside the tube must be heated before use. For best results, place the tubes in a heating pad to melt the candy inside the tubes; this allows the chocolate to heat slowly without scorching.

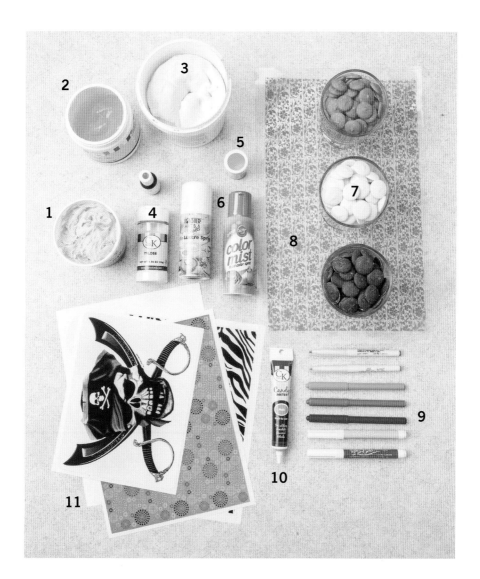

## EDIBLE FROSTING SHEETS

Edible frosting sheets (11) are blank sheets of edible paper or pictures printed on edible paper with food color. Blank edible sheets are available in full sheets or in circles. Printed sheets are available in full sheets, strips, or pre-printed themed designs for the top of a cake. Some cake supply stores offer to print customer's pictures. If printing pictures taken by a professional photographer, or if copyright information is written on the back, seek the photographer's permission before printing the image. Begin by

covering the cake with white buttercream or white rolled fondant. Colored icings show through the white areas and will likely change the tints of the colored areas of the frosting sheet. Frosting sheets work on icings, but do not work on chocolate coatings. Use chocolate transfer sheets for printed designs on chocolate candy-coated treats. Keep frosting sheets tightly sealed in a plastic bag at room temperature. If the sheet is difficult to remove from the paper backing, place it in the freezer for a few minutes.

# Baking a Cake and Cupcakes

A WELL-BAKED CAKE that tastes great will make your beautifully decorated cake even better. Mixing a cake from scratch can be a bit time consuming but is rewarding. This book does not provide cake recipes. Find recipes by visit baking websites or ask a loved one to share a favorite cake recipe. Store-bought cake mixes are another alternative. Such mixes produce delicious, moist cakes and are convenient for beginning decorators. Simply follow the instructions on the cake mix box. The instructions on the boxes from major baking companies are clear, concise, and easy for children to follow.

## BAKING A CAKE

Follow these general baking instructions for most cake pans. Dozens of shapes, sizes, and pan materials can be found in cake decorating supply stores. Novelty cake pans are available in several themes and popular licensed characters.

1. Preheat the oven according to the recipe's instructions. Using a pastry brush, generously spread pan grease thoroughly in the pan. Pan grease is available at cake and candy supply stores. If pan grease is unavailable, substitute solid vegetable shortening and then dust with all-purpose flour.

**2.** Prepare the cake batter according to the recipe's instructions. Pour the batter into the cake pan, filling the pan just over half full.

**3.** Place the filled pan in the preheated oven on the center rack. Bake according to the recipe's instructions. Check to see if the cake is done by inserting a cake tester into the center of the cake. If the cake tester comes out clean or with a few cake crumbs, the cake is done. If the tester comes out with batter, the cake is not thoroughly baked. Leave the cake in the oven and test after a minute or two. After the cake is baked, remove the pan from the oven and place on a cooling rack. Allow the cake to cool in the pan for 10 minutes. After cooling for 10 minutes, run a knife along the edge of the pan to loosen the sides.

**4.** When the pan is cool enough to handle, place a second cooling rack on top of the cake pan, sandwiching the pan between the cooling racks. Hold on to the two cooling racks tightly and flip over the pan.

**5.** Place the cooling racks on the counter and remove the top cooling rack. Gently lift the cake pan. Allow

*More to Know*

A single-layer cake is a cake baked and then decorated. These cakes are typically 1½" to 2" (3.8 to 5.1 cm) tall. A two-layer cake is a cake with two baked cakes placed on top of one another, usually with filling in between the layers. Two-layer cakes are generally 3" to 4" (7.6 to 10.2 cm) tall.

the cake to cool completely before decorating, or the icing will melt.

**6.** If the cake is domed, use a cake slicer to cut off the top of dome.

*Important*

• Thoroughly grease and flour the cake pan to prevent the cake from sticking to the pan when you are trying to release it. Extra grease and flour should be used on cake pans with embossed designs. Before releasing the cake from the pan, allow the pan to cool about 10 minutes. The pan should be warm, but not hot. If the cake is released too soon after baking, the cake may crack. If too much time passes before removing the cake, the cake may stick to the pan.

• If the cake has a sunken middle, the cake is likely underbaked. If the cake did not rise while baking, the batter may have been overmixed. Opening the oven door during baking may also cause the cake to deflate.

| Sheet Cakes | Number of Servings | Cake Batter Needed | Filling Needed |
|---|---|---|---|
| 9" x 13" (23 x 33 cm) (quarter sheet cake) | 20 | 6 cups (1.5 L) | 1½ cups (375 mL) |
| 11" x 15" (28 x 38 cm) | 25 | 10 cups (2.3 L) | 2½ cups (625 mL) |
| 12" x 18" (30 x 46 cm) (half sheet cake) | 36 | 13 cups (3 L) | 3½ cups (875 mL) |

| Round cakes | Number of servings | Cake Batter Needed | Filling Needed |
|---|---|---|---|
| 6" (15 cm) | 8 | 1¼ cups (300 mL) | ⅓ cups (75 mL) |
| 7" (18 cm) | 10 | 1¾ cups (425 mL) | ⅔ cups (150 mL) |
| 8" (20 cm) | 18 | 2½ cups (625 mL) | ¾ cups (175 mL) |
| 9" (23 cm) | 24 | 2¾ cups (675 mL) | 1 cup (250 mL) |
| 10" (25 cm) | 28 | 4¼ cups (1 L) | 1¼ cups (300 mL) |
| 12" (30 cm) | 40 | 5½ cups (1.4 L) | 1¾ cups (425 mL) |

| Square Cakes | Number of Servings | Cake Batter Needed | Filling Needed |
|---|---|---|---|
| 6" (15 cm) | 12 | 2¼ cups (550 mL) | ¾ cup (175 mL) |
| 7" (18 cm) | 16 | 3½ cups (875 mL) | ⅔ cup (150 mL) |
| 8" (20 cm) | 22 | 4 cups (1 L) | 1 cup (250 mL) |
| 9" (23 cm) | 25 | 5½ cups (1.375 L) | 1¼ cup (300 mL) |
| 10" (25 cm) | 35 | 7 cups (1.75 L) | 1½ cup (375 mL) |
| 12" (30 cm) | 50 | 10 cups (2.3 L) | 2 cups (500 mL) |

## CAKE CHART

The numbers and quantities in the following chart are provided as an estimate and are meant to be used as a general guide. Requirements and results will vary according to the user.

## Number of servings

The number of servings will depend entirely on how large or how small the cake is cut. A 12" × 18" (30 × 46 cm) sheet cake will serve 54 if the pieces are cut into 2" (5 cm) squares, or 36 if the pieces are cut into 2" × 3" (5 × 7.5 cm) rectangles. The number of servings for the sheet cake is based on a one-layer cake. The number of servings for round and square cakes is based on a two-layer cake. When deciding what size cake to bake, bigger is better. It is better to have extra than to run out of cake.

## Cake batter

One standard cake mix contains four to six cups of batter. The charts for the amount of batter needed are based on filling a single pan that is 2" (5 cm) tall, filling ⅔ full with cake batter. Filling the pan with less than ⅔ batter may produce a cake that is too thin.

| Icing Needed | Fondant Needed | Bake Temp | Bake Time |
|---|---|---|---|
| 6 cups (1.5 L) | 40 ounces (1 kg) | 350°F (175°C) | 35–40 min |
| 8 cups (2 L) | 60 ounces (1.7 kg) | 325°F (160°C) | 35–40 min |
| 10 cups (2.3 L) | 80 ounces (2.2 kg) | 325°F (160°C) | 45–50 min |

| Icing Needed | Fondant Needed | Bake Temp | Bake Time |
|---|---|---|---|
| 3 cups (750 mL) | 18 ounces (0.5 kg) | 350°F (175°C) | 25–30 min |
| 3½ cups (875 mL) | 21 ounces (0.6 kg) | 350°F (175°C) | 23–32 min |
| 4½ cups (1.125 L) | 24 ounces (0.7 kg) | 350°F (175°C) | 30–35 min |
| 5 cups (1.25 L) | 30 ounces (0.9 kg) | 350°F (175°C) | 30–35 min |
| 5½ cups (1.375 L) | 36 ounces (1 kg) | 350°F (175°C) | 35–40 min |
| 6½ cups (1.6 L) | 48 ounces (1.3 kg) | 350°F (175°C) | 35–40 min |

| Icing Needed | Fondant Needed | Bake Temp | Bake Time |
|---|---|---|---|
| 4 cups (1 L) | 24 ounces (0.7 kg) | 350°F (175°C) | 25–30 min |
| 4¾ cups (1.2 L) | 30 ounces (0.9 kg) | 350°F (175°C) | 25–32 min |
| 5 cups (1.25 L) | 36 ounces (1 kg) | 350°F (175°C) | 35–40 min |
| 5¾ cups (1.4 L) | 42 ounces (1.1 kg) | 350°F (175°C) | 35–40 min |
| 6½ cups (1.6 L) | 48 ounces (1.3 kg) | 350°F (175°C) | 35–40 min |
| 8 cups (2 L) | 72 ounces (2 kg) | 350°F (175°C) | 40–45 min |

## Fillings

The amount of filling needed may fluctuate depending on the type of filling used. The cake charts are based on a thin layer of pastry filling. If a thick, fluffy filling is used, such as buttercream, the amount of filling required should be doubled.

## Icing

The amount of icing needed is based on icing the cake with the buttercream icing recipe included in this book. The amount of icing needed will vary according to consistency, thickness applied, or if other recipes are used. The figures for the amount of icing needed include enough icing for piping a border or simple piped accents. The amount of icing needed for the sheet cake is based on a one-layer cake. The amount of icing needed for the square and round cake is based on a two-layer cake.

## Rolled Fondant

The figure for the amount of fondant needed includes just the amount needed for covering the cake and does not include additional decorations. This amount can vary significantly depending on the thickness of the rolled fondant.

## BAKING CUPCAKES (see images above)

Hundreds of baking cups are available in many themes and colors. If a dark cake is used, the baking cup design may not be visible. It is best to use white cake batter if you want the design on the baking cup to show. A scoop is a useful tool when filling cupcake cavities. It keeps the filling process clean while scooping even amounts into each cavity. Use a 2-ounce scoop for standard cupcakes. Use a ⅓ cup scoop for jumbo cupcakes.

**1.** Line a cupcake pan with baking cups. Follow the recipe's instructions for preheating the oven and mixing the cake batter. Use a cookie scoop to fill the baking cups. The cups should be a little over half full.

**2.** Place the filled cupcake pan in the preheated oven and bake according to the recipe's instructions. Set the timer for 18 minutes or according to the recipe instructions. Check to see if the cupcakes are done by inserting a cake tester into the center of a cupcake. If the cake tester comes out clean or with a few cake crumbs, the cupcakes are done. If the tester comes out with batter, the cupcakes are not thoroughly baked. Leave the cupcakes in the oven and test within another minute or two or until the cake tester comes out clean. After the cupcakes are baked, remove the pan from the oven and place the pan on a cooling rack. Allow the pan to cool for 10 minutes. When the pan is cool

enough to handle, remove the cupcakes and place them on a cooling rack. Allow the cupcakes to cool completely before decorating, or the icing will melt.

## ADDING COLOR TO CAKE BATTER (see images on facing page)

Adding color to cake batter is an easy way to create a fun, vibrant surprise when the cake or cupcake is cut. Start with a white cake mix or white cake recipe. Use electric gel food colors for the brightest cakes.

**1.** Follow instructions for mixing the cake batter, using a white cake recipe or a white cake mix. Stir in food color. Pour the batter into the pan.

**2.** Make each layer a different color for an awesome presentation when the cake is cut.

**3.** If more than one color is desired, separate the batter into bowls for however many colors are desired. You can use several bowls and add color to each to make bright and colorful rainbow cupcakes. Add a scoop of each color until the baking cup is filled just over half full.

**4.** Enjoy your colorful creation!

| Cupcakes (based on one cake mix) | Amount of Filling Needed | Icing Needed: Spread | Icing Needed: Piped | Bake Temp | Bake Time |
|---|---|---|---|---|---|
| 96 mini cupcakes | 1 cup (250 mL) | 4 cups (1 L) 2 tsp. (10 mL) per cupcake | 6 cups (1.5 L) 1 Tb. (15 mL) per cupcake | 350°F (175°C) | 8–10 min |
| 24 standard cupcakes | 1 cup (250 mL) | 3 cups (750 mL) 2 Tb. (25 mL) per cupcake | 4½ cups (1.125 L) 3 Tb. (50 mL) per cupcake | 350°F (175°C) | 18–24 min |
| 7 jumbo cupcakes | 3/4 cup (175 mL) | 1½ cups (375 mL) 3 Tb. (50 mL) per cupcake | 2 cups (500 mL) 4 Tb. (59 mL) per cupcake | 350°F (175°C) | 20–25 min |

## CUPCAKE CHART

The chart above is based on cupcakes made from one standard cake mix which contains four to six cups (960 mL to 1.4 L) of batter and will bake approximately 96 mini cupcakes, 24 standard cupcakes, or 7 jumbo cupcakes. Cupcakes will take less icing if the icing is spread on the cupcake versus icing piped with a tip. If additional details will be piped with icing, double the amount of icing needed. All of the figures are approximate.

# Filling Cakes and Cupcakes

SURPRISE YOUR GUESTS by using a filling in the cake or cupcakes. The filling can be buttercream icing (or your favorite icing), pastry fillings (available at cake supply stores), or even ice-cream toppings such as hot fudge.

## FILLING A CAKE

1. Fill a pastry bag with buttercream icing the same color that will be used on the outside of the cake. With tip #1A, pipe a dam of icing around the edge of the bottom layer of the cake. This dam will prevent the filling from oozing out the sides.

2. Squirt filling in the center of the cake. Spread the filling to the edges of the dam.

3. Aligning the layer, gently place the top layer on the bottom layer of cake.

## More to Know

*An apple corer is an ideal size to fill a standard size cupcake (left). Also shown is a cupcake plunger that works well for a jumbo size cupcake (right).*

### FILLING CUPCAKES

1. Allow the baked cupcakes to cool completely. When the cupcakes are cool, use a cupcake corer or an apple corer (shown) to remove the center of the cupcakes.

2. Press the trigger of the cupcake corer, or use the apple corer press to release the cut center.

3. Fill a pastry bag fitted with tip #2A with your favorite filling. Pipe the filling into the hollowed center of the cupcake, filling almost to the top.

# Buttercream and Rolled Fondant Basics

BUTTERCREAM AND ROLLED FONDANT are used on the cake, cookie, and cupcake projects throughout this book. Buttercream is a fluffy, sweet icing that is either spread onto the cake or treat with a spatula or piped into fun textures or shapes using a pastry bag fitted with a cake decorating tip. Rolled fondant is a sweet, chewy icing that is rolled flat using a rolling pin and then formed over the cake or cut to fit a cookie or cupcake. Using rolled fondant is similar to working with clay. It can be cut into fun shapes, hand molded, or rolled in strips to form bows, loops, or stripes. When creating your own projects, use either icing or a combination of the two. For example, if the theme cake is covered in rolled fondant and has accents with rolled fondant, but you prefer the flavor of buttercream, simply ice the cake with buttercream and decorate it with rolled fondant accents.

## BUTTERCREAM ICING

Buttercream is a traditional icing that is very sweet and fluffy. The icing will crust on the outside, but remain creamy on the inside. Buttercream is available premade at cake supply stores, or follow the recipe. The recipe includes hi-ratio shortening, which is available from specialty bakery supply stores and online sources. Baker's (hi-ratio) shortening is a shortening produced to replace butter. Use it instead of solid vegetable shortening to produce an icing with a fine, smooth, and creamy texture without a greasy aftertaste. Solid vegetable shortening may affect the icing consistency. For a bright white buttercream, choose clear butter and vanilla flavor. Pure vanilla will give the icing an ivory hue. Do not whip the icing on medium or high speed after the ingredients are blended. Doing so will add extra air into the icing, causing bubbles.

## Buttercream Recipe

½ cup (120 mL) high-ratio shortening

4 cups (520 g) powdered sugar, sifted

5 tablespoons (75 mL) water

½ teaspoon (2.5 mL) salt

1 teaspoon (5 mL) vanilla flavoring

½ teaspoon (2.5 mL) almond flavoring

¼ teaspoon 1.5 mL) butter flavoring

In a large bowl, combine the ingredients; beat on low speed until well blended. Continue beating on low speed for 10 minutes or until very creamy. Keep the bowl covered to prevent the icing from drying out. Unused icing can be kept in the refrigerator up to 6 weeks. Rewhip stored icing on low speed before using.

## Chocolate Buttercream Recipe

Make a delicious chocolate buttercream icing simply by adding cocoa powder to the buttercream recipe. Add 1 cup (110 g) of cocoa powder to the buttercream recipe above. The cocoa powder may cause the buttercream to stiffen. Add a small amount of water to achieve the desired consistency.

## Storing Buttercream

Cakes that are iced and decorated with buttercream will most likely form a crust. Humidity may affect the icing's ability to crust. An iced and decorated cake with buttercream can be kept at room temperature for three or four days. Extreme warm temperatures can cause the icing to soften and melt. Refrigerating iced and decorated cakes with buttercream may cause condensation, making colors bleed.

## ROLLED FONDANT

Rolled fondant is used to cover cakes and to create accents. The icing has a chewy texture. Before covering a cake with fondant, the cake should have an undericing. Icing the cake first in buttercream gives the cake a smooth base while adding sweetness and sealing in moisture. Recipes are available for making rolled fondant, but it can be difficult to achieve the proper texture. Before attempting a recipe, try using commercial rolled fondant to become familiar with the texture and consistency. The flavor of commercial rolled fondant will vary tremendously. Gum paste is used to make accents that hold up better than rolled fondant. Gum paste sets very hard and should not be eaten. Purchase commercial gum paste, or make an easy gum paste by kneading 1 tablespoon of food-grade tylose into rolled fondant. Wrap the tylose gum paste tightly and allow the paste to rest for several hours. Use candy clay, page 52, as an alternative to rolled fondant for accents on cakes but not as a cake covering. All forms of edible clay including rolled fondant, gum paste, and candy clay will dry out quickly. Keep the edible pastes tightly wrapped and sealed when not working with them.

### Rolled Fondant Recipe

½ (120 g) cup cream

2 tablespoons 30 mL) unflavored gelatin

¾ (175 mL) cup glucose

2 tablespoons (28 g) butter

2 tablespoons (25 mL) glycerin

2 teaspoons (10 mL) clear vanilla flavor

2 teaspoons (10 mL) clear butter flavor

1 teaspoon (5 mL) clear almond flavor

approximately 9 cups (1 kg) powdered sugar

Pour the cream into a small saucepan. Sprinkle gelatin on the cream and cook on low until the gelatin has dissolved. Add the glucose, butter, glycerin, and flavorings. Heat until the butter is melted. Set aside. Sift the powdered sugar. Place 7 cups (770g) of the powdered sugar in a mixing bowl. Pour the cream mixture over the powdered sugar and mix slowly with a dough hook until the powdered sugar is thoroughly mixed. Add the additional 2 cups (220g) of powdered sugar. The fondant will be very sticky, but should hold its shape. Lay a sheet of plastic wrap on the counter, and coat with a thin layer of vegetable shortening. Wrap the fondant in the greased plastic wrap and allow to set for 24 hours. After 24 hours, the fondant should be less sticky. If not, add more powdered sugar.

### Rolling Rolled Fondant for Cutting Accents

Dust the work surface with powdered sugar. Knead and soften the rolled fondant. Roll the fondant, lifting and turning it after every other roll. If the fondant is sticking to the surface, add more powdered sugar. Do not flip the rolled fondant over. Use perfection strips to keep the rolled fondant an even thickness. The rolled fondant should be rolled using the thinnest strips (2 mm thick) for accents on cakes. Daintier accents should be rolled thinner than 2 mm. A pasta machine is ideal for rolling fondant very thin to make dainty accents. Use medium strips (4 mm) when covering cookies with rolled fondant.

# Food Color

ROLLED FONDANT AND BUTTERCREAM icing are available pre-colored at cake supply stores for convenience. Purchasing icing pre-colored keeps your hands and clothing free of food color stains. However, it may be more cost effective to purchase white icing and add color using food colors. Concentrated colors such as gel colors and powder colors are best suited for coloring icings and fondant. If using liquid food color, excessive color may be needed, which may affect the consistency of the buttercream and rolled fondant. Even when using gels or powdered colors, it can be difficult to obtain dark colors such as red, brown, and black. The shade of each tube or jar of food color will vary from pale to deep depending on the amount of color added to the icing. Too much color and the icing may taste bitter and may also leave a tinge on mouths when eaten. When mixing black or brown, begin by adding cocoa powder to the icing to achieve a brown base; this will eliminate the need to add excessive amounts of black or brown food color. When mixing red, start with a no-taste red and add a vibrant red, such as super red. If mixing powdered colors into the buttercream or rolled fondant, blend a small amount of vegetable shortening with the powdered food color. When coloring chocolate candy coating, use an oil-based food color. Water-based coloring will cause the chocolate to thicken.

Food color will stain clothes, countertops, and hands. Wear aprons when adding food color to avoid staining clothing. Water and soap will remove coloring from hands, although it may take several washings. Use bleach or powdered cleanser on countertops to remove stains. Test an unseen area of the counter top first.

Colors may fade if the decorated cake is exposed to light. Natural sunlight and fluorescent lights will produce the harshest effects, but even common household lighting may cause the colors on the cake to fade. Keep the cake in a cool, dark room to avoid fading. Storing the cake in a covered box will also reduce the fading.

When moisture affects the icing, colors may bleed. Keep iced cakes in a loosely wrapped box until ready to serve. An airtight container will cause condensation to form, which may cause bleeding. Placing a cake in the refrigerator may also cause the colors to bleed. When piping on icing, allow contrasting colors to form a crust before adding an adjoining color.

## ADDING COLOR TO ROLLED FONDANT
### (see images below)

Excessive color may cause the rolled fondant to become sticky. Knead in additional powdered sugar if the food color changes the consistency. Avoid using liquid food color, as it requires a significant amount of coloring to obtain bright colors. Concentrated gel or powdered coloring works best.

**1.** Knead and soften the rolled fondant. With concentrated food color, add a dot of color.

**2.** Knead until there are no streaks of color remaining.

## ADDING COLOR TO BUTTERCREAM ICING
### (see images above)

Dark colors in buttercream icing may intensify upon setting. Allow the icing to set for 2 or 3 hours to see true color.

**1.** Add a small amount of food color to the icing. Use a toothpick to remove color in jars, or if the color is in tubes, squeeze the color into the icing.

**2.** Blend until all color is thoroughly incorporated. There should be no streaks of color. If the color is too dark, add white icing. If the color is too light, add a little more color.

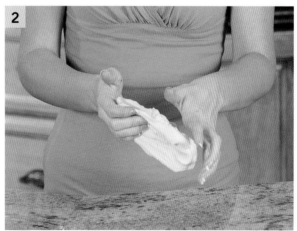

# Icing Cakes and Cupcakes

## ICING A CAKE

It takes practice and patience to ice a cake with a smooth, clean finish. Place the cake on a turntable to help you manipulate the spatula with consistent pressure. First apply a crumb coat, which seals the crumbs and prevents them from mixing with the buttercream. When crumb coating, use two bowls; one for icing that is free of crumbs, and the other to scrape the spatula as you remove excess icing and crumbs.

1. Place the cake on a cardboard the same size as the cake. Mix icing for the crumb coat by thinning buttercream with a small amount of water (about 1 teaspoon of water to 1 cup of buttercream). It should be just thin enough to barely see crumbs underneath. Spread the thinned icing on the cake, also covering the cardboard. Allow the crumb coat to form a crust (20–45 minutes). Dispose of left-over thinned icing.

2. After the crumb coat has set, place a generous amount of buttercream icing on the top of the cake.

3. With a long spatula, spread the icing on the top using long strokes and gliding toward the edge.

4. Apply icing to the side of the cake, holding the spatula perpendicular to the turntable. Blend the icing on the top with the icing on the sides.

5. Glide the spatula along the top and sides of the cake to smooth.

6. After the icing forms a crust (approximately 45 minutes), gently roll over any areas that are not smooth with a pastry roller.

## ICING CUPCAKES

Icing can be spread or piped onto cupcakes. When piping cupcakes, use an icing that holds its shape, such as buttercream, or the details will be lost. Refer to the icing chart on page 25 to determine how much icing is needed.

### Piping Icing onto Cupcakes (see images below)

**1.** Allow the cupcake to cool completely. Fit a pastry bag with a tip that has a large opening. Tips #1A, #1M, or #8B work well for piping icing onto cupcakes. Fill the pastry bag with buttercream icing. Pipe a ring around the outside edge of the cupcake. Continue piping, creating a swirl on top of the cupcake.

**2.** Each tip gives a unique piped design as shown, left to right: #1M, #1A, #8B.

### Spreading Icing onto Cupcakes (see images above)

**1.** Scoop a generous amount of icing onto the top of a baked and cooled cupcake.

**2.** Evenly spread the icing to the edges of the cupcake.

# Covering Cakes and Cupcakes with Rolled Fondant

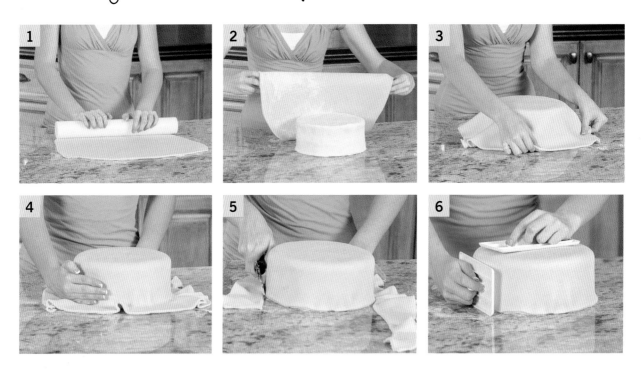

## COVERING A CAKE WITH ROLLED FONDANT

Covering a cake with rolled fondant provides a smooth, clean appearance. Try to complete all the steps within 5–7 minutes. The fondant may develop tiny cracks or "elephant skin" if too much time elapses. An undericing provides extra sweetness and a clean, smooth surface. The instructions are for a cake with buttercream underneath, but other icings may be used. To allow the cake to be easily moved after it is covered, place it on a cardboard the same size as the cake. Powdered sugar or cornstarch can be used on the countertop to keep the fondant from sticking. When working with children, use powdered sugar, as it will blend into the fondant; cornstarch does not blend and will cause white powdery spots on the fondant. Too much cornstarch can also quickly dry out the fondant. When rolling fondant, be sure to rotate it often so fondant holds an even shape. Avoid flipping the fondant, as residue from the countertop will stick to the fondant.

1. Bake and cool the cake. Place the cake on a cardboard the same size. With thinned buttercream, crumb coat the cake; then ice the cake following instructions on page 32. After the buttercream has crusted, brush the top with piping gel. Dust the work surface with powdered sugar. Knead and soften the rolled fondant. Roll the fondant, lifting and turning the fondant every other roll. If the fondant is sticking to the surface, add additional powdered sugar. Do not flip the rolled fondant over. Continue rolling until the fondant is approximately ⅛" (3 mm) thick. Roll out a circle of fondant so it is the diameter of the cake plus the height of the cake doubled plus 1" (2.5 cm); this will provide enough fondant to cover the cake even if the fondant is not perfectly centered. For example, the cake shown is 8" (20.3 cm) in diameter and 4" (10.2 cm) tall. The amount of rolled fondant needed is 8 + 4 + 4 + 1 = 17" (20.3 + 10.2 + 10.2 + 2.5 cm = 43.2 cm).

**2.** Lift the rolled fondant using the rolling pin. Starting at the base of the cake, unroll the fondant onto the cake.

**3.** Lift and shift the sides to eliminate any creases. Take care not to stretch and pull the fondant.

**4.** Secure the edges by pressing palms against the sides of the cake.

**5.** With a mini pizza cutter, remove any excess fondant.

**6.** With your nondominant hand, rest one fondant smoother on the top of the cake to hold the cake steady and to smooth the top of the cake. Do not apply pressure or the smoother will impress lines. Smooth the sides with another fondant smoother. Spread buttercream on a cake plate or cake cardboard. Lift the cake using a jumbo spatula and place on the cake plate.

### COVERING CUPCAKES WITH ROLLED FONDANT
Add a smooth finish to cupcakes with rolled fondant. Rolled fondant is a bit heavy for a handheld treat, so be sure to roll the fondant thin when covering cupcakes. A thin layer of buttercream icing underneath the fondant adds additional sweetness. A 3" (7.6 cm) round cookie cutter will cover cupcakes with a slight dome. Cupcakes that are slightly underfilled or overfilled will require a smaller or larger disk of fondant. It is helpful to have a set of round cookie cutters with a range of sizes.

**1.** Bake and cool the cupcakes. Fit a pastry bag with tip #2A. Fill the bag with buttercream or any icing that can be piped. Pipe a swirl on the cupcake, leaving approximately ½" (1.3 cm) all around the edge. Dust the work surface with powdered sugar. Knead and soften the rolled fondant. Roll the fondant, lifting and turning the fondant every other roll. If the fondant is sticking to the surface, add additional powdered sugar. Do not flip the rolled fondant over. Continue rolling until the fondant is approximately ⅛" (3 mm) thick. Use a cookie cutter to cut circles. Place the cut circles on top of the just-iced cupcakes. Smooth the top and sides of the covered cupcake with your palm.

*Important*

### CIRCUMFERENCE AND DIAMETER
*It is often necessary to determine the circumference or diameter of round cakes. For accuracy, measure after icing a cake or covering a cake with rolled fondant. For example, after an 8" (20 cm) cake is covered with fondant, it may have a diameter of 8¼" (21 cm).*

**Diameter:** *The diameter is the line that passes through the center of a circle. Most round cake pans are measured by their diameter. An 8" (20 cm) cake pan will be 8" (20 cm) in diameter.*

**Circumference:** *The circumference is the measurement around the cake. This figure is important to know when wrapping fondant ribbon strips or adding a decorative ribbon around the cake board. The circumference is figured by taking the diameter of the pan (or board) and multiplying it by 3.14 (or π).*
*An 8" (20 cm) cake has a circumference of 25.1" (64 cm). If wrapping a cake with a fondant ribbon, 25.1" (64 cm) will be required.*

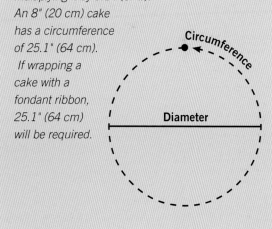

Circumference

Diameter

# Cake Boards and Cake Stands

CAKE STANDS AND FANCY CAKE PLATES allow you to present your decorated cakes in an attractive way. If using a decorative stand, place the baked cake on a cardboard the same size as the cake and decorate the cardboard as though it were part of the cake. This keeps the cake plate free of knife scratches when serving. Cardboards or cake drums (page 10) can be used instead of a cake stand or cake plate. The boards should be at least 1" (2.5 cm) larger than the cake to allow for a border and make it easier to move. Cardboards should be covered with cake foils (available at cake supply stores) both for additional elegance and to keep the fats in the cake and icings from soaking through the cardboard. Cake cardboards or cake drums can also be covered with rolled fondant that perfectly coordinates with the cake.

## COVERING A CARDBOARD WITH FOIL

If a cardboard is not covered, oils from the cake and icing may soak through the cardboard. FDA-approved cake foil is available at cake supply stores. Aluminum foil wrinkles and tears easily and is not the best covering for the cardboards.

**1.** Place the cardboard on the foil. Cut the foil so it is slightly larger than the cardboard.

**2.** Fold over the long sides first and secure with tape. Fold all four corners in a triangle.

**3.** Fold over the short side and secure with tape. Use additional tape if necessary.

**4.** Turn completed cardboard over. It is now ready to use.

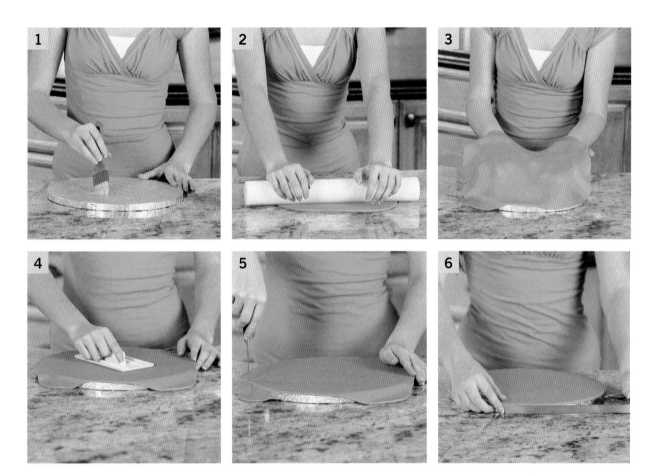

## COVERING A CARDBOARD WITH ROLLED FONDANT

Covering a board with rolled fondant provides a harmonizing cake design from top to bottom. For best results, cover the board with rolled fondant at least a day before you plan to place the cake on the covered board; this allows the fondant to become more durable and less likely to be smudged or scratched when placing the cake on top.

**1.** Brush piping gel on the cake cardboard.

**2.** Knead and soften the rolled fondant. Roll the fondant, lifting and turning the fondant every other roll. If the fondant is sticking to the surface, add more powdered sugar. Do not flip the rolled fondant over. Continue rolling until the fondant is approximately ⅛" (3 mm) thick. Be sure enough fondant is rolled to cover the diameter of the board.

**3.** Lift the fondant and place it on the cake cardboard covered with piping gel.

**4.** Use a fondant smoother to smooth the rolled fondant.

**5.** Hold a paring knife perpendicular to the board and cut away excess rolled fondant.

**6.** Using fabric glue, add a ribbon around the edge of the cake board if desired.

# Stacking a Cake

MAKE YOUR CAKE EXTRA SPECIAL by adding tiers. It is important to stack cakes properly, or the weight from the upper tiers will cause the cake to collapse. Cakes should not be stacked on one another without support. Plates and dowel rods are necessary between each tier. Choose plastic plates or cardboards that are grease-resistant. Plain cardboards will absorb grease and may become unstable.

**1.** Insert a dowel into the bottom tier of the cake. The dowel should go completely through the cake and rest on the base board. Mark the height of the cake.

Remove the dowel. The dowels should be placed toward the center of the cake so the top of the dowels will not be visible when the top tier is placed on top.

**2.** With a serrated knife or a hacksaw, cut four dowels the same height as the marked dowel. Insert the cut dowels into the cake

**3.** Use a cake lifter to pick up the top tier. Position the top tier in the center and gently set on top of the bottom tier.

# Using Pastry Bags

CLEAR, DISPOSABLE PASTRY BAGS are ideal for children to use, as they can see all the colors to choose from and there is little cleanup when finished. Reusable pastry bags are also available. The tips of the bags can be cut and a cake decorating tip dropped in. One-third of the tip should be showing. If more than one-third is showing, the bag may tear. A coupler can be used to change tips without filling a new bag. If only one tip is needed for a single color, it is not necessary to use a coupler; however, a coupler does keep icing from seeping. When children are using pastry bags, be sure to secure the pastry bag with a rubber band or icing bag tie to prevent the icing from bursting from the top of the bag.

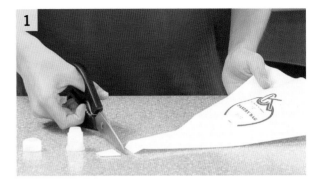

## USING A COUPLER

1. Cut the reusable pastry bag or disposable pastry bag so that 1 or 2 threads are showing on the coupler base when the coupler base is dropped into the bag.

2. Drop the coupler into the bag. Pull the coupler tightly to secure. Place the tip on the coupler base. Twist the coupler screw top to tighten the tip in place.

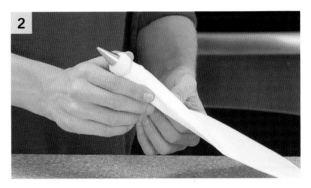

## FILLING PASTRY BAGS

3. Drop the tip into the pastry bag or fit the pastry bag with a coupler and tip following instructions above. Fold the pastry bag over hands to form a cuff. The cuff fold should be 2" to 3" (5.1 to 7.6 cm). Scoop icing into the bag until it reaches the top of the cuff. Fill the bag about half full with icing. The more full the bag, the more difficult the bag is to control.

4. Squeeze the bag between your thumb and fingers and push the icing toward the bottom of the bag. Twist the bag where the icing begins. To control the icing, grip the bag with your dominant hand. Use the tip of your index finger on your nondominant hand to guide the bag. Squeeze the icing while guiding the bag.

# Piping Using Tips

ADD TEXTURE to cookies, cakes, and cupcakes by piping designs with icing. An icing that holds its shape, such a buttercream, is a must. Successful piping depends on using the right amount of consistent pressure. Practice on a sheet of parchment paper using various amounts of pressure. It is important to keep the tip clean and free of icing buildup for crisp and precise piping. If piping a border on a cake, place the cake on a turntable and rotate to achieve an even, consistent border.

## DOTS

Use piped dots for polka dots, flower petals, flower centers, or a dot border. The most popular tips for piping dots are #2, #3, #4, #6, #8, and #10. However, it is handy to have nearly every round-opening tip. The smaller the number, the smaller the piped dot.

**1.** Start with the pastry bag at a 90° angle just above the surface. Squeeze the pastry bag to pipe a dot, holding the tip steady as the icing forms around the tip. Continue squeezing the pastry bag until the dot is the desired size. Stop pressure and lift the pastry bag.

**2.** If there are small peaks after the dots are formed, gently press the peak with the tip of your index finger just before the icing forms a crust.

## STARS AND FLOWERS

Use piped stars for simple piped accents and easy borders. Stars are also commonly used on shaped theme cakes. Pipe stars close together to completely cover the cake. The most popular tips for piping stars are #16, #18, #21, and #32. The smaller the number, the smaller the piped star.

**3.** Start with the pastry bag at a 90° angle just above the surface. Squeeze the pastry bag to pipe a star, holding the tip steady as the icing forms around the tip.

Continue squeezing the pastry bag until the star is the desired size. The bag should not be lifted until the star is formed. Stop pressure and lift the pastry bag.

**4.** Make a flower by adding a small dot in a contrasting color to the center.

## LEAVES

Tips #350, #352, and #366 (large leaf) are used to pipe leaves. These tips look like a bird beak. When piping, remember to have 1 point of the "bird beak" on the work surface. Do not pipe with the "bird beak" on its side.

**5.** Position the pastry bag at a 45° angle. One point of the tip should be touching the surface. Squeeze the pastry bag with a short burst of pressure to attach the leaf. Gradually release pressure and lift the tip. Stop pressure and lift the pastry bag.

## GRASS

Tip #233 is used to pipe grass or fur. When piping grass, be sure the tip is kept clean, or the strands will come out in a blob. Most metal grass tips have ridges around the fine holes. The ridges make it difficult to keep the end of the metal tip clean. The plastic grass tip is smooth without ridges, which makes it easier to keep clean. The length and style of grass can vary. To pipe long strands of grass, attach grass with a burst of pressure. Continue with a lot of pressure while lifting.

**6.** Position the pastry bag at a 90° angle. The tip should be touching the surface. Squeeze the pastry bag with a short burst of pressure to attach the grass. Continue with pressure and drag the tip upward. Stop pressure and lift the pastry bag. Pipe the grass close together so there are no gaps.

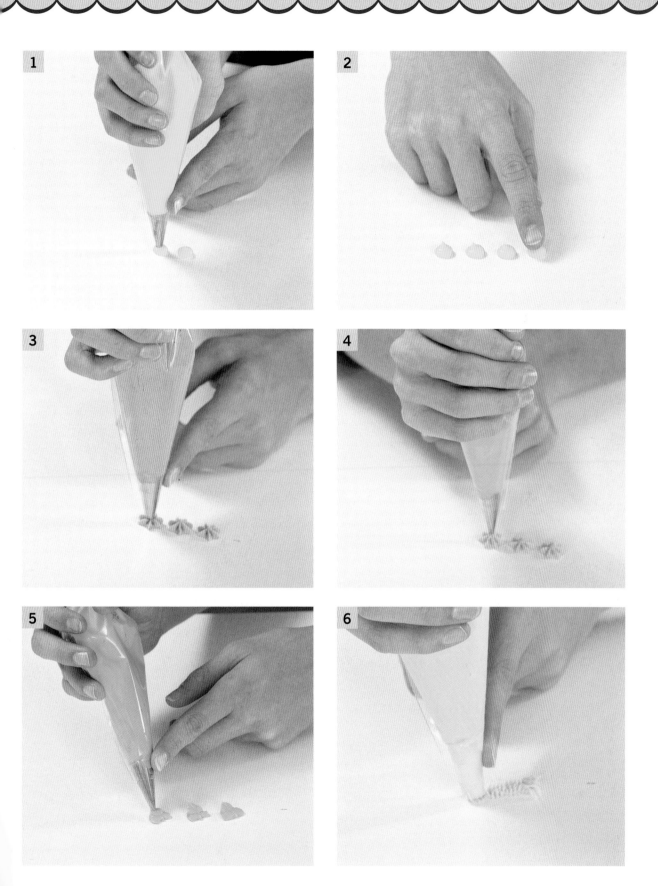

uninterrupted pressure, piping a line or curve for the letter or number. Let the icing flow from the bag naturally just above the surface. Do not drag the tip on the cake. Stop pressure and touch the surface to attach the end of the letter or number.

## SHELL BORDER

A shell border is the most common border used on cakes. Tip #21 produces a border with deep groves, while tip #32 creates a border with finer grooves. Use tip #18 for smaller, daintier borders.

8. Position the pastry bag at a 45° angle, nearly touching the surface. Apply pressure while moving the tip forward slightly. Move back to the starting point, gradually release pressure, and drag the tip to form a shell. Stop pressure and pull the tip away. Start the next shell at the tail of the first shell.

## TEARDROP BORDER

Use a tip with a round opening, such as tip #10, to form a teardrop-shaped border. Tip #12 will produce a larger designed border, while tip #8 (shown) will create a daintier border.

9. Position the pastry bag at a 45° angle, nearly touching the surface. Squeeze the pastry bag to form a ball. Gradually release pressure and drag the tip to form a teardrop. Start the next teardrop at the end of the first teardrop.

## ZIGZAG BORDER

Use a star tip to pipe this fun border. You can vary the design simply by piping the points closer together or by stretching the distance between the points. Use tip #18 for a nice size zigzag border.

10. Position the pastry bag at a 45° angle, nearly touching the surface. With steady pressure move the tip in a zigzag pattern. When the border is complete, stop applying pressure and lift the pastry bag.

## WRITING

Use a tip with a round opening, such as tip #2, #3, or #4, for writing on the cake. The smaller the tip number, the daintier the writing. If the lines are breaking when piping, you are not applying enough pressure or are moving the piping bag too fast. If too much pressure is applied, the lines may have wiggles or loops.

7. Position the pastry bag at a 45° angle. Squeeze the pastry bag to release the icing, touch the surface, and then lift the icing just above the surface while continuing with pressure. Continue piping with

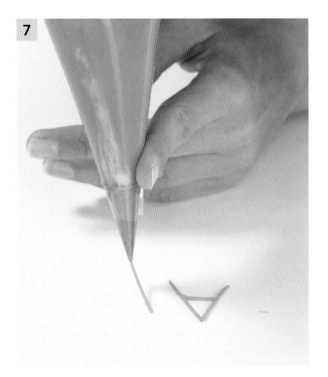

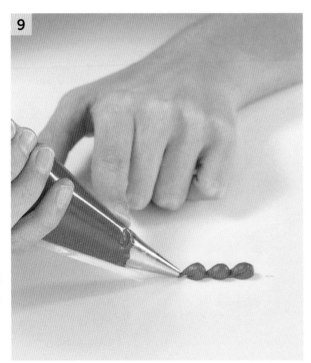

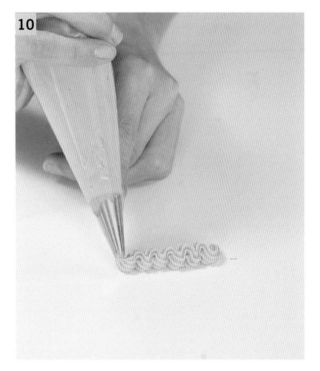

# Rolling and Baking Cookies

CUTOUT COOKIES are not just for the holidays. Decorate shaped cookies to coordinate with the party cake. Cookie cutters are available in hundreds of shapes. Plastic cutters are great to use for younger children because there are no sharp edges. Metal cutters are most commonly available in tin, stainless steel, and copper. Copper cutters tend to be formed thicker, making them less sharp than other metals.

## COOKIE RECIPES

The two recipes included in this chapter have a subtle sweetness that is enhanced with icing. Both cookies have a tender crumb; not too soft and not too crisp. The Buttery Sugar Cookie recipe must be chilled at least 2 hours before rolling to firm the cream cheese and butter. The Chocolate Cutout Cookie recipe can be used immediately after mixing. The chocolate cookie tends to crumble a bit when rolling, and the cookies can easily be overbaked because the edges do not brown. Baked cookies, with or without icing, are best eaten within 7 to 10 days.

### Buttery Sugar Cookie

1 cup (2 sticks [225 g]) unsalted butter, softened

3 ounces (85 g) cream cheese, softened

¾ cup (170 g) sugar

1 egg

1 teaspoon (5 mL) vanilla

3 cups (330 g) all-purpose flour

Combine the butter and cream cheese with an electric mixer on medium speed for 2 or 3 minutes or until well blended. Scrape the sides of the bowl.

Add the sugar. Continue to blend on medium speed until the mixture is light and fluffy. Add the vanilla and mix.

Add the egg, mixing on low until thoroughly blended. Scrape the bowl.

Add the flour, 1 cup (110 g) at a time. Scrape the bowl after adding each cup. Mix until just incorporated. Do not overmix, or the dough will toughen.

Divide the dough into two equal portions. Flatten the dough into two patties that are approximately 1½" (3.8 cm) thick. Wrap the patties with plastic wrap and refrigerate at least 2 hours or until firm.

Preheat the oven to 375°F (190°C). Roll out the dough and cut the cookies (page 45). Bake the cookies for 9 to 11 minutes or until the edges are very lightly browned.

*Yields 36 (3" to 4" [7.6 to 10.2 cm] cookies)*

### Chocolate Cutout Cookies

1 cup (2 sticks [225 g]) butter, softened

1½ cup (340 g) sugar

2 eggs

2 teaspoons (10 mL) vanilla

3 cups (330 g) all-purpose flour

⅔ cup (75 g) unsweetened cocoa powder

½ teaspoon (2.5 mL) salt

Preheat the oven to 350°F (175°C). In a large bowl, stir together the flour, cocoa powder, and salt.

In a separate large bowl, combine the butter and sugar with an electric mixer on medium speed for 2 or 3 minutes or until the mixture is light and fluffy. Scrape down the sides of the bowl.

Add the eggs and vanilla and mix on low until thoroughly blended. Scrape the bowl.

Add the flour mixture, 1 cup (110 g) at a time. Scrape the bowl after adding each cup of flour. Mix until just incorporated. Do not overmix, or the dough will toughen.

Divide the dough into two equal portions. Flatten the dough into two patties that are approximately 1½" (3.8 cm) thick. Use the dough immediately, or refrigerate until ready to mold or roll.

Bake the cookies for 8 to 10 minutes or until no indentation is made when touched.

*Yields 36 (3" to 4" [7.6 to 10.2 cm] cookies)*

## ROLLING COOKIE DOUGH AND CUTTING SHAPES

A baked cookie provides a smooth surface for icing. Use perfection strips or a rolling pin with rings (page 11) to achieve a cookie with an even surface. The icing used determines how thick the baked cookie should be. If the baked cookie is thin and the buttercream on the cookie is piled high, the buttercream will overpower the cookie. If covering the cookie in rolled fondant, the baked cookie should be at least twice as thick as the rolled fondant piece. For best results, the dough should be cool, but not too cold that it is difficult to roll. Take the dough out of the refrigerator an hour before rolling it.

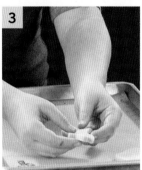

1. Chill dough, if required in recipe. Place the cookie dough between perfection strips on the countertop dusted with flour. Roll over the strips, leveling the cookie dough. The dough may also be rolled on a silicone mat or a sheet of parchment paper. If the dough is sticking to the parchment paper, silicone mat, or countertop, lightly dust with as little flour as possible to avoid toughening the dough. If the dough is still sticking, try chilling the dough for 1 or 2 hours. If it is still sticking, you can add more flour to the dough, but it may toughen the baked cookie.

2. Press the cutter into the dough, cutting the shapes as close together as possible.

3. Remove the excess dough and transfer the cut shape to a cookie sheet lined with a silicone mat or parchment paper.

4. Bake the cookies according to the recipe instructions. After the cookies are baked, allow the cut shapes to cool approximately 3 to 4 minutes. Use a cookie spatula to gently transfer the warm, cut shapes to a cooling rack. Baked cookies will be fragile and soft to touch while they are still hot. Take extra care when transferring the baked cookie from the cookie sheet to the cooling rack. Allow the cookies to cool completely before decorating.

5. To insert a stick into cookies to make a cookie bouquet, follow steps 1–3 above. Insert the stick into the dough. Rest the stick on the cookie sheet at the base of the cookie dough. Hold the other end of the stick between the index finger and thumb of your dominant hand, and begin twisting and pushing the stick up into the cut cookie dough. Keep the stick as parallel to the cookie sheet as possible. Use the index finger of your nondominant hand to keep the stick from protruding through the cookie dough. Push until the stick is about three-fourths into the cut shape. Continue with step 4 above. If the cookie becomes loose from the stick after baking, add a bit of icing or melted chocolate coating to the back of the cookie, securing the stick.

# Icing Cookies

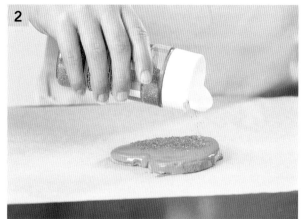

THREE ICINGS are covered in this chapter: chocolate coating, buttercream icing, and rolled fondant. A cookie coated in chocolate coating gives a delicious, smooth covering. Because the chocolate coating sets firm, these cookies are great for stacking. If the cookies are served outside and it is warm, the chocolate coating may melt. Buttercream icing on a cookie provides a sweetness like no other. Buttercream can also be piped onto cookies using the piping techniques on pages 40–43. Rolled fondant gives a covering with a clean, professional finish.

## DIPPING A COOKIE IN CHOCOLATE COATING

1. Melt candy coating following directions on page 48. Hold on to the cookie and dip the top into the melted candy coating. After lifting the cookie out of the coating, turn your wrist so the coated cookie is facing you. Tap your wrist against the counter to smooth the chocolate coating.

2. Place the cookie on parchment paper to set. If sprinkles are desired, add them before the chocolate coating sets.

3. Smaller cookies may be immersed in the chocolate coating and then removed using a dipping tool.

## COVERING A COOKIE WITH ROLLED FONDANT

**4.** Bake and cool cookies. Brush the top of the cookie with a very thin layer of piping gel. Knead and soften the rolled fondant. Dust the work surface with powdered sugar. Roll the fondant in between perfection strips, lifting and turning the fondant after every other roll. If the fondant is sticking to the surface, add more powdered sugar. Do not flip the rolled fondant over. Continue rolling until the fondant is approximately 2 to 4 mm thick. The baked cookie should be twice as thick as the rolled fondant or the rolled fondant will overpower the cookie. Cut the fondant with the same cutter used for the cookie.

## ICING A COOKIE WITH BUTTERCREAM

**5.** Scoop a generous amount of buttercream onto the cookie. Spread the icing across the cookie using a spatula at least the length and width of the cookie. Clean the spatula.

**6.** Hold the spatula perpendicular to the cookie and scrape along the side to clean the edge of the cookie.

# Coordinating Party Treats

IMPRESS YOUR GUESTS by making delicious treats to coordinate with the cake or to give as party favors. Many of these treats are made with candy coating which is easy to use. Simply melt in the microwave and dip your treat into the melted candy. Chocolates and coatings have a very low melting point, so watch it carefully as it melts to prevent scorching. Using a bowl with a squared edge allows the chocolate coating to be easily poured into squeeze bottles. Small tubes filled with candy coating are called candy writers—use them to paint suckers or add details to cookies. This chapter covers coating pretzels and sandwich cookies, but almost any snack can be dipped in chocolate. Try graham crackers, popcorn, nuts, or even potato chips!

## MELTING CANDY COATING

1. Place the candy wafers in a microwave-safe bowl. Put the bowl in the microwave. Turn on the microwave for 30 seconds. Remove the bowl from the microwave and stir. Put the bowl of wafers back into the microwave and turn on for 20 more seconds. Remove the bowl from the microwave and stir again.

2. Continue in this way by heating for 20 seconds, removing the bowl, and then stirring until all but a few wafers have melted. Stir until the unmelted wafers melt.

## More to Know

- Keep the bowls of melted chocolate, filled squeeze bottles, parchment cones, and candy writers warm by placing them in an electric skillet on the lowest setting lined with several dry towels. The skillet should be warm to touch but not hot enough to burn or the chocolate will cook and burn instead of melt. Bottles and candy writers can also be placed in a heating pad set to low to keep the chocolate warm.

- A wide variety of colored candy coating can be purchased ready to use. If a color is desired that is not available, simply color the candy with an oil-based food color. Avoid using food color gels, pastes, and liquids, or the chocolate may thicken when color is added. You can use powdered food colors, but be sure to dissolve the powder in liquid vegetable shortening before adding to the chocolate.

## GENERAL MOLDING (see images below)

1. Use candy writers to paint details inside of candy molds. Allow the candy to set at room temperature before adding adjoining colors. Only use candy writers to paint details. Do not use them for filling the entire cavity. The chocolate candy inside candy writers must be heated before using the tube. Place the candy writer tube in a heating pad for 1 hour before using. Keep the candy writers in the heating pad to prevent the candy from setting up in between use. If the tip of the candy writer clogs, use a straight pin to unclog.

2. Allow the details to set up at room temperature. Pour melted candy coating into a squeeze bottle. After the details have set, fill the rest of the mold using the candy from the squeeze bottle. Place the filled molds in the freezer to set. The time needed for the candy to set is determined by the thickness of the mold cavity. Thin candy pieces set up after a few minutes in the freezer, while thick pieces will take much longer. The candy should release from the mold with little effort.

## CHOCOLATE SUCKERS (see images above)

1. Follow steps 1 and 2 for General Molding at left. Insert a sucker stick at least three-fourths into the filled cavity. Place the filled mold in the freezer for a few minutes.

2. When the suckers are ready, the candy will feel cold and the mold will be cloudy. Place a towel on the countertop. Turn over the sucker mold onto the towel to release the suckers. If the candy sticks to the mold when the mold is turned over, the candy is not ready. Return the mold to the freezer. If the candy cracks or breaks when the mold is turned over, the candy was left in the freezer too long.

## CHOCOLATE-DIPPED PRETZEL TWISTS

**1.** Melt candy wafers. Place the pretzel twist into the melted candy coating, using a dipping fork to immerse completely. Use the dipping fork to lift the pretzel twist out of the melted candy coating. Tap the dipping fork against the bowl to allow excess candy to drip off of the pretzel.

**2.** Set the dipped pretzel on a sheet of parchment paper. Immediately add sprinkles. Allow the pretzel to harden at room temperature.

## More to Know

*A chocolate transfer sheet can be used to quickly add color and designs onto a cookie. Cut the transfer sheet into squares that are slightly larger than the cookies. Immediately after the cookies are dipped, place a transfer sheet, textured side down, onto the dipped cookie. It is important to place the transfer sheet on the dipped cookie right away before the chocolate sets.*

*Allow the candy to set for at least 15 minutes. After 15 minutes, peel back the transfer sheet.*

## CHOCOLATE DIPPED PRETZEL RODS

**1.** Melt candy wafers. Hold on to one end of the pretzel rod. Use a spoon to coat the pretzel with the melted candy. Turn the pretzel and continue to coat until all but the end you are holding is covered with melted candy.

**2.** After the pretzel is coated, tap the uncoated end of the pretzel on the bowl to allow excess candy to drip off of the pretzel. Set the dipped pretzel on a sheet of parchment paper. Immediately add sprinkles. Allow the pretzels to harden at room temperature.

## CHOCOLATE-DIPPED SANDWICH COOKIES

**1.** Melt candy wafers. Place the sandwich cookie into the melted candy coating, using a dipping fork to immerse completely. Use the dipping fork to lift the cookie out of the melted candy coating. Tap the dipping fork against the bowl to allow excess candy to drip off of the cookie.

**2.** Set the dipped cookie on a sheet of parchment paper. Immediately add sprinkles, sugar decoration, or icing decoration before the candy sets.

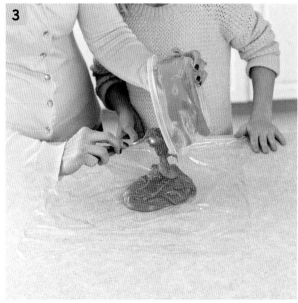

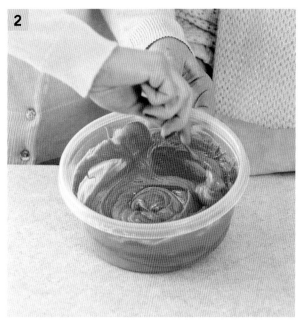

## CANDY CLAY

Candy clay is a simple combination of melted chocolate and corn syrup. This edible chocolate clay can be used in place of rolled fondant for most projects, though it is not ideal for covering a cake. Use it to shape or cut hand-molded accents. Or use candy clay instead of Styrofoam as a filler when making bouquets.

**1.** Lay out a long sheet (approximately 24" [61 cm]) of plastic wrap on the work surface. Melt the chocolate candy coating. Stir in ⅔ cup (5.3 oz) corn syrup.

**2.** The mixture will immediately begin to thicken. Stir until the corn syrup is thoroughly mixed.

**3.** Pour the thickened mixture onto the center of the plastic wrap. Tightly wrap the mixture. Allow the candy clay to set for several hours to become firm. After the candy clay becomes firm, knead to soften again before working with the candy clay.

## CAKE BALLS

Cake balls are a popular party treat. It is important to use the proper amount of icing with these goodies—too much icing and the shape of the ball will not hold; too little icing and the cake ball will crumble and fall apart. One cake mix will make approximately 18 to 24 cake pops sized 1" to 2" (2.5 to 5.1 cm).

1. Bake and cool any flavor of cake. Place the baked and cooled cake in a bowl. Crumble the cake with your hands until the cake becomes coarse crumbs.

2. Add a small amount of icing to the bowl. Blend the icing in with your hands. The amount of icing needed will vary depending on the moistness of the cake. Typically only 1 or 2 tablespoons of icing will be needed. Add just enough icing so that the cake holds together when squeezed without being sticky.

3. Roll the cake mixture into cake pops. Form balls, egg shapes, or any other shape desired. Place the cake pops into the freezer for at least an hour.

4. Insert a stick into the firm cake pop. Spoon melted candy coating over the cake pop. Rotate the stick to ensure the pop is completely coated. Hold the pop over the melted candy coating bowl and rotate the stick, allowing excess candy coating to drip off the pop. Continue rotating the stick until the candy coating on the pop is nearly set. Insert the stick into a block of Styrofoam to continue to firm.

# Party Themes

Now that we have covered the basics, the following chapters will present ideas and instructions to create treats in popular party themes. Follow these instructions and ideas exactly, or use them for inspiration and follow the techniques shown to decorate beautiful cakes, cookies, and cupcakes with your own colors and themes. Projects are graded with one, two, or three hands. One hand means the project is easy. Three hands means the project is more difficult and may be better suited for older children. In most cases, one-hand projects are quick, while three-hand projects are more time consuming. Most projects also include suggestions for involving younger kids. The amount of icing or rolled fondant required will vary depending on the creator. Use the charts on page 22, 23 and 25 for an estimate on how much icing or rolled fondant is needed for each project.

# Soccer Cake and Cookies

## SOCCER BALL CAKE

### You Will Need

soccer ball cake pan

9" (22.9 cm) cardboard

10" (25.4 cm) round cake pan

12" (30.5 cm) cake drum or
cake plate

rolled fondant, blue, pink,
and orange

flower plunger cutter

flower former

disposable pastry bags

6 cups (1.5 L) buttercream icing,
electric green

¼ cup (60 mL) buttercream icing,
gray

1 cup (250 mL) buttercream icing,
black

3 cups (750 mL) buttercream icing,
white

tip #233

tip #18

tip #4

piping gel

### Techniques

Baking Cakes, page 20

Icing Cakes, page 32

Cake Boards and Cake Stands,
page 36

Buttercream and Rolled Fondant
Basics, page 28

Piping Using Tips, page 40

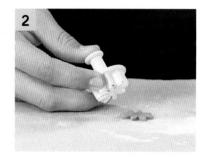

1. At least one day ahead of time, make the flowers for the cake. Dust the work surface with powdered sugar. Roll kneaded and softened rolled fondant thin. Using a flower plunger cutter, firmly press into the rolled fondant, holding the base of the cutter—do not hold onto the plunger when cutting.

2. Lift the cutter and gently run your finger along the edge of the cutter to ensure the cut is clean. Push the trigger to release the cut flower. If the cut flower remains on the work surface, use a spatula with a thin blade to lift it. Dust the surface with additional powdered sugar before cutting more flowers.

## Important

*The flowers around the buttercream grass border and on the soccer cookies should be made ahead of time. Or buy premade edible flowers, available at most cake decorating supply stores.*

## More To Know

*Shaped cake pans, such as the soccer pan used here, are available in a variety of themes as well as popular television and movie characters. To decorate these cakes, use buttercream icing to outline shapes and then pipe stars to fill them in.*

# SOCCER BALL CAKE *(continued)*

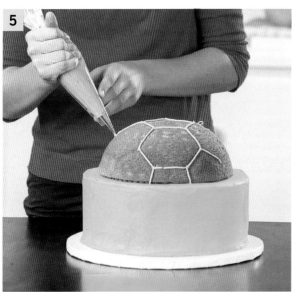

## Younger Kids

*Give a spatula to younger kids to stir all the different colors of buttercream. Be sure the kids are wearing an apron, as the colors may stain their clothes. The rolled fondant edible flowers can be made by kids of all ages. Kids can also place the flowers on the cookies and cake.*

**3.** Place the cut flower in a flower former tray to shape the petals. Add a dot of piping gel in the center of the flower and place a candy bead or Sixlet in the center of the flower.

**4.** Bake a two-layer 10" (25.4 cm) round cake, following instructions on pages 20–23. Ice the cake with electric green buttercream, following instructions on pages 32. Place the cake on a 12" (30.5 cm) board. Bake a cake using a soccer ball cake pan. Allow the cake to cool completely. Place the soccer ball cake on a 9" (22.9 cm) cardboard circle or a cardboard the same size or slightly smaller than the soccer ball. Gently place the cake onto the iced 10" (25.4 cm) cake.

**5.** Fit a pastry bag with tip #4. Fill the bag with gray icing. Outline the cake. To outline, touch the cake and gently squeeze the pastry bag to attach the icing. Continue squeezing, gently lift the bag, and pipe a line following the indentations shown on the baked cake. Stop pressure and touch the cake to attach the icing. Outline the entire cake.

**6.** Fit two pastry bags with tip #18. Fill one bag with black icing and the other with white icing. Fill in the outlined soccer ball with stars piped close together. To pipe a star, hold the pastry bag just above the cake. Squeeze the bag to pipe a star. Continue squeezing the bag until the star is the desired size. Stop pressure and lift the bag. Pipe the stars side by side and very close together so there aren't any gaps that will show the cake underneath. Pipe the next row of stars between previously piped stars to eliminate gaps.

**7.** Fit a pastry bag with tip #233. Fill the bag with electric green icing. Pipe grass around the base of the soccer ball and around the bottom of the 10" (25.4 cm) cake. To pipe grass, hold the pastry bag at a 90° angle. The tip should be touching the iced cake. Squeeze the pastry bag with a short burst of pressure to attach the grass. Continue applying pressure and drag the tip upward. Stop pressure and lift the pastry bag. Pipe the grass close together to eliminate gaps.

**8.** Press rolled fondant flowers or premade flowers into the cake.

## SOCCER BALL COOKIES

**You Will Need**

soccer cookie cutter texture set

rolled fondant in white and in colors desired for flowers (or use other edible flowers)

piping gel

food color marker, black

**Techniques**

Rolling and Baking Cookies, page 44

Rolled Fondant Basics, page 28

Icing Cookies, page 46

1. At least one day ahead of time, make the flowers for the cookies following steps 1–3 on pages 57–58 Bake and cool round cookies on a stick using the cutter from the soccer ball cookie cutter texture set. Roll the white fondant thin. Place the smooth, rolled side of the fondant on top of the soccer ball texture mat. With a lot of pressure, roll over the fondant.

2. Turn over the fondant and peel back the mat.

3. Use the same cutter that was used for baking the cookies to cut the soccer ball design.

4. Brush the cookie with a thin layer of piping gel. Place the cut fondant soccer ball on top of the cookie.

5. Allow several hours for the fondant to harden. When the fondant is firm, color in the textured details using a black food color marker.

6. Use piping gel to attach the edible flowers to the cookies.

### More To Know

*Some cookie cutters, such as the soccer ball, come with plastic mats with recessed lines that line up with the cutter. Use the mats to add texture and instant details to rolled fondant.*

# Shabby Chic Sweet 16

★ ★ ★

## SHABBY CHIC CAKE

### You Will Need

7" (17.8 cm) cake pan

7" (17.8 cm) waxed cake board

9" (22.9 cm) cake pan

9" (22.9 cm) waxed cake board

dowel rods

9 cups (2.2 L) buttercream icing

rolled fondant in pink, lime green, and aqua

4 edible frosting sheets

piping gel

tip #18

mini pizza cutter

#1 and #6 cookie cutters, size 3" (7.6 cm)

### Techniques

Baking Cakes, page 20

Icing a cake, page 32

Stacking a cake, page 38

Cake boards and Cake stands, page 36

Buttercream and Rolled Fondant Basics, page 28

Piping Using Tips, page 40

**1.** At least one day ahead of time, make the numbers for the top of the cake. Dust the work surface with powdered sugar. Roll kneaded and softened rolled fondant ⅜" (1 cm) thick. Remove the edible sheet from the paper baking. Brush the back of the edible sheet with piping gel.

**2.** Place the edible sheet on the rolled fondant. Gently smooth the edible paper.

**3.** Cut the numbers using cookie cutters. Insert a toothpick at the base of the number. Gently twist, inserting half of the toothpick into the number. Allow the numbers to harden overnight.

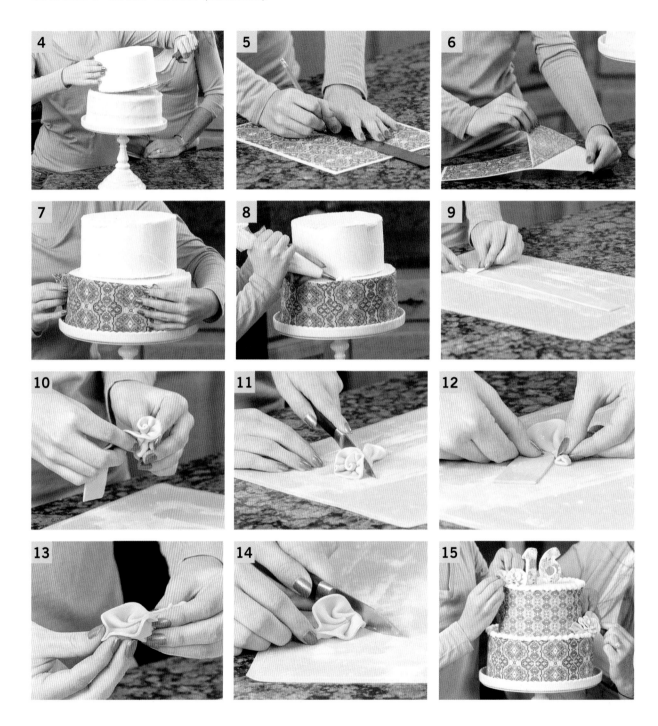

## More to Know

*Edible frosting sheets can be cut to fit the cake or cookies. Six full-size sheets will cover a 7" and 9" (17.8 and 22.9 cm) cake (both 4" [10.2 cm] tall) and 18, 3" (7.6 cm) cookies.*

**4.** Bake a two-layer 7" (17.8 cm) round cake and a two-layer 9" (22.9 cm) round cake, following the instructions on pages 20–21. Ice both cakes with white buttercream (page 32). Place the 9" (22.9 cm) cake on a cake board or a cake stand. Insert dowel rods into the 9" (22.9 cm) cake and place the 7" (17.8 cm) cake on top, following instructions for stacking a cake on page 38.

**5.** Measure the height of the cake. With the edible frosting sheet still on its paper backing, cut the sheet the height of the cake. The cake shown is 4" (10.2 cm) tall, so the strips were cut 4" (10.2 cm). It takes 3 strips to wrap around the 9" (22.9 cm) cake and 2¼ strips to wrap around the 7" (17.8 cm) cake.

**6.** With the pattern facing up, slide the edible frosting sheet over the edge of a countertop to loosen the sheet. Peel the edible frosting sheet from the paper backing. Brush the back of the strip with piping gel.

**7.** Gently wrap the strip around the cake. Add additional strips so that the entire side of the cake is covered.

**8.** Pipe a shell border using white buttercream in a bag fitted with tip #18.

**9.** Dust the work surface with powdered sugar. Roll kneaded and softened rolled fondant thin. Using a mini pizza cutter, cut a 1" × 12" (2.5 × 30.5 cm) strip of rolled fondant. Fold the end of the strip at an angle.

**10.** Begin rolling the strip. Keep the base pinched and allow the petals to expand.

**11.** After the rose is formed, it will have a thick base. Cut the excess rolled fondant from the base.

**12.** Dust the work surface with powdered sugar. Roll the kneaded and softened rolled fondant thin. Using a mini pizza cutter, cut a 1" × 6" (2.5 × 15.2 cm) strip of rolled fondant. Start in the center and pleat the rolled fondant like a fan until one side is completely folded into the middle.

**13.** Pleat the other side. Pinch the base of the leaf; then gently press the top of the leaf.

**14.** Cut the excess rolled fondant from the base.

**15.** Brush piping gel on the bottom of the numbers. Insert the hardened numbers into the center of the cake. Attach the leaves and the roses to the cake with piping gel.

## Important

- *Edible frosting sheets are thin and very delicate. Be careful to use a gentle touch when applying the edible sheet. If the sheet tears, gently press the design back together if possible.*

- *The numbers for the top of the cake should be made at least a day ahead of time to allow them to harden. If the humidity is high, the flowers and leaves for the cupcakes and cake should also be made at least a day ahead of time.*

## ★ ★

# SHABBY CHIC COOKIES

**You Will Need**

edible frosting sheets

rolled fondant, white

piping gel

3½" (8.9 cm) fluted round
 cookie cutter

**Techniques**

Rolling and Baking Cookies,
page 44

Rolled Fondant Basics , page 28

Icing Cookies, page 46

**1.** Bake and cool cookies using a fluted round cookie cutter.

**2.** Dust the work surface with powdered sugar. Roll kneaded and softened white rolled fondant thin.

**3.** Remove the edible frosting sheet from the paper baking. Brush the back of the edible sheet with piping gel. Place the edible sheet on the rolled fondant.

**4.** Cut the patterned rolled fondant using the same cookie cutters used in baking. Brush the cookie with a thin layer of piping gel. Place the pattered rolled fondant piece on top of the piping gel covered cookie.

## *Coordinating Treats*

*Chocolate-covered pretzels (page 50) accent the cake and cookies. Sandwich cookies dipped in several pastel colors are adorned using a chocolate transfer sheet printed with a white floral pattern (page 50).*

# SHABBY CHIC CUPCAKES

★★

## You Will Need

standard cupcake pan

buttercream icing, white

rolled fondant in pink, lime green, and aqua

mini pizza cutter

tip #1M

cupcake wrappers

## Techniques

Baking cupcakes, page 24

Icing cupcakes, page 33

Buttercream and Rolled Fondant Basics, page 28

**1.** At least several hours ahead of time, make ribbon roses and leaves following steps 9–15 on page 64. For smaller roses, roll 1" × 6" (2.5 × 15.2 cm) strips. For smaller leaves, roll 1" × 4" (2.5 × 10.2 cm) strips. Bake and cool cupcakes following directions on page 24. Add filling, if desired, following directions on page 27. Drop the cupcakes into cupcake wrappers. Pipe buttercream icing on the cupcakes using a pastry bag fitted with tip #1M.

**2.** Add a ribbon rose and leaf.

## Younger Kids

*Allow little ones to drop the cupcakes into the wrapper and place the ribbon roses and leaves on the cupcakes. They can brush piping gel on the cookies and set the cut patterned rolled fondant piece in place.*

## More to Know

*Cupcake wrappers showcase a design on the side of the cupcake better than baking cups. The cupcakes are baked using coordinating baking cups. After the cupcakes are baked and cooled, they are slipped into cupcake wrappers and then decorated. If the wrappers are not grease-proof, oils from the icing may soak into the wrappers. Ice the cupcakes just before serving if the wrappers are not grease-proof.*

# Monster Bash

★★

## MONSTER CUPCAKES

### You Will Need

standard cupcake pan

buttercream icing, white

tip #1M

edible frosting sheet 2" (5.1 m) circles

2" (5.1 cm) round cookie cutter

rolled fondant, white

food color markers

piping gel

### Techniques

Baking cupcakes, page 24

Icing Cupcakes, page 33

Buttercream and Rolled Fondant Basics, page 28

## Important

*Prepare the circles for the top of the cupcakes at least a day ahead of time to allow the circles to firm and not distort when placed on the iced cupcakes.*

1. At least one day ahead of time, draw and color monsters on the edible frosting sheet circles using food color markers.

2. Dust the work surface with powdered sugar. Roll kneaded and softened white rolled fondant thin. Remove the edible frosting sheet circles from the paper baking. Brush the rolled fondant with piping gel. Peel back the drawn and colored circles from the paper backing. If the edible circles are sticking, slide the edible frosting sheet over the edge of a countertop to release the circles.

3. Place the edible circles on the rolled fondant. Cut the circles using a round cookie cutter the same size or slightly larger than the edible circles. Place the cut circles on parchment paper and allow to set for several hours or overnight.

4. After the circles have hardened, pipe buttercream icing on the cupcakes using a pastry bag fitted with tip #1M. Place the rolled fondant circles on the cupcakes.

# MONSTER COOKIES

**You Will Need**

edible frosting sheet 3" (7.6 cm) circles

3" (7.6 cm) round cookie cutter

buttercream icing, white

tip #2A

food color markers

**Techniques**

Rolling and Baking Cookies, page 44

Buttercream Basics, page 28

**1.** Bake and cool round cookies that are the same size or slightly larger than the frosting sheets. With a black food color marker, draw monsters on the edible frosting sheet circles. Use food color markers and color in the details. Peel back the drawn and colored circle from the paper backing. If the edible sheets are sticking, slide the edible frosting sheet over the edge of a countertop to release the circles.

**2.** Fit a pastry bag with tip #2A. Fill the pastry bag with white buttercream icing. Pipe icing onto the cookie. Place the edible sheet on the iced cookie.

## More to Know

Edible frosting sheets come both in full-size sheets that can be cut to fit nearly any project and in individually precut circles, which is what is used in this project. Edible frosting sheets are thin and very delicate. Take care to use a gentle touch when applying the edible sheet. If the sheet tears, gently press the design back together if possible. Keep the sheets covered until ready to use.

## Younger Kids

Children of all ages can create patterns or pictures using food color markers on blank edible frosting sheets. Then the kids can place the colored circles on top of the rolled fondant for the cupcakes or on top of the iced cookies.

# Pretty Pony

★★★

## PRETTY PONY CAKE

### You Will Need

14" × 11" (35.6 × 27.9 cm) oval pan

large rectangle cake cardboard

rolled fondant in dark ivory, light pink, dark pink, light brown, and dark brown

buttercream icing

2½" (6.4 cm) flower cutter

flower former

extruder

1" × 1⅜" (2.5 × 3.5 cm) oval cutter

5" (12.7 cm) heart cutter

piping gel

powdered sugar

### Techniques

Baking Cakes, page 20

Covering Cakes with Rolled Fondant, page 34

Cake boards and Cake stands, page 36

Rolled Fondant Basics, page 28

1. At least one day ahead of time, make the flower for the cake. Dust the work surface with powdered sugar. Roll kneaded and softened light pink rolled fondant thin. Cut the flower and place in a flower former. These petals are delicate. Make an extra flower or two to allow for breakage. Allow the flowers to harden overnight.

2. At least one day ahead of time, make the ears for the cake. Dust the work surface with powdered sugar. Roll kneaded and softened dark ivory rolled fondant thin. Cut the fondant using a heart-shape cutter. Cut the

## Important

- *The horse's ears and the flower for the cake should be made a day ahead of time. The brim of the cowboy hat cake pop should also be made at least a day ahead of time, but three or four days would be ideal.*

- *The cake board should be covered at least a day ahead of time to allow the rolled fondant to firm to avoid imprinting the rolled fondant.*

**2**

**3**

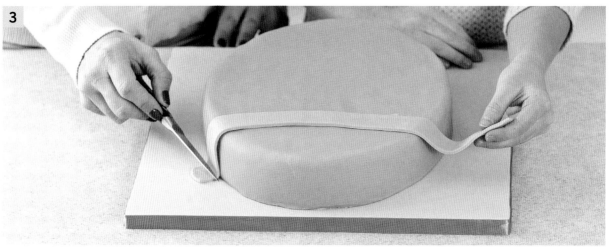

**4**

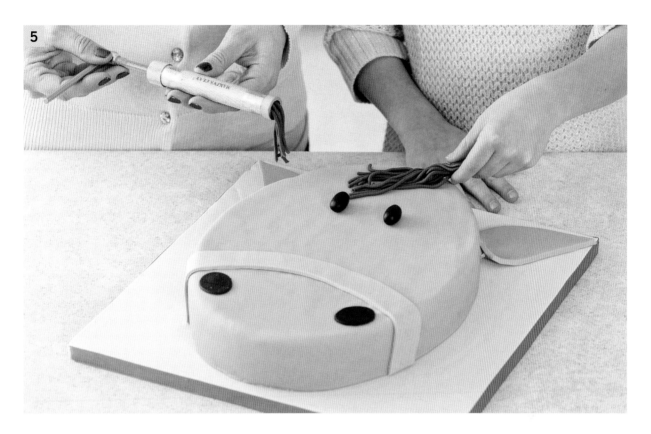

5

heart in half down the middle. Pinch the wide part of the heart. Allow the ears to harden overnight.

3. At least one day ahead of time, cover a cake board with light pink rolled fondant. Bake an oval cake, following instructions for baking on page 20. This size of cake will take about 1½ cake mixes to get a 2" (5.1 cm) tall cake. Allow the cake to cool completely. Cut a cardboard to fit the cake using the cake pan as a template. Place the baked and cooled cake on the cardboard. Ice the cake and the cardboard with buttercream. Cover the cake with dark ivory rolled fondant. Place the cake on the rolled fondant–covered cardboard. Roll kneaded and softened dark pink rolled fondant thin. Use a pizza cutter and cut a long strip of fondant, approximately 1" × 14" (2.5 × 35.6 cm) for the horse's bridle. Place the bridle on the cake, attaching with piping gel.

4. Roll kneaded and softened dark brown rolled fondant thin. Cut the fondant using an oval cutter. Attach to the cake with piping gel. Roll dark brown fondant into an oval shape for the eyes. Attach to the cake with piping gel.

5. Arrange the ears and attach to the cake board using piping gel. Form a snake with light brown rolled fondant. Feed the snake into an extruder fit with a disk that has several round openings. Extrude the rolled fondant until it is long enough for the horse's mane. Add the mane to the cake, attaching with piping gel. Add the flower using piping gel to attach. Roll dark pink fondant in a ball for the center of the flower. Attach the center with piping gel.

# PRETTY PONY COOKIES

### You Will Need

rolled fondant in dark ivory, light pink, dark pink, light brown, and dark brown

4" (10.2 cm) egg cookie cutter

6 mm strip cutter

flower plunger cutter

extruder

8 mm oval cutter

1" (2.5 cm) small heart cutter

piping gel

powdered sugar

### Techniques

Rolling and Baking Cookies, page 44

Icing cookies, page 46

Rolled Fondant Basics, page 28

1. Bake and cool egg-shaped cookies. Roll kneaded and softened dark ivory rolled fondant thin. Cut the fondant using the egg cutter that was used for baking the cookies. Brush piping gel on the cookie. Place the cut dark ivory fondant on the cookie. Knead and soften the dark ivory rolled fondant. Roll the fondant thin. Cut out a heart. Cut the heart in half down the middle. Pinch the wide end of the heart. Attach to the cookie with piping gel.

2. Roll kneaded and softened dark pink rolled fondant thin. Cut the fondant using a strip cutter. Lift 1 strip and place it on the horse's nose for the bridle. Attach with piping gel.

## Younger Kids

*Younger kids can brush piping gel on the cookie and place the rolled fondant piece on the top. Allow younger children to arrange the horse face features on the cookies and cake. The small flowers on the cookies and cowboy hat cake pops are easy for little kids to cut and plunge.*

**3.** Roll kneaded and softened dark brown rolled fondant thin. Cut out small ovals and attach them to the cookie with piping gel.

**4.** Form a snake with light brown rolled fondant. Feed the snake into an extruder fit with a disk that has several tiny round openings. Extrude the rolled fondant until it is long enough for the horse's mane. Add the mane to the cookie, attaching with piping gel.

**5.** Dust the work surface with powdered sugar. Roll kneaded and softened light pink rolled fondant thin. Firmly press a flower plunger cutter into the rolled fondant, holding the base of the cutter—do not hold on to the plunger when cutting. Lift the cutter and gently run your finger along the edge of the cutter to ensure the cut is clean. Push the trigger to release the cut flower. If the cut flower remains on the work surface, use a spatula with a thin blade to remove the flowers. Dust the surface with additional powdered sugar before cutting more flowers. Add the flower using piping gel to attach. Roll the dark pink fondant in a ball for the center of the flower. Attach the center with piping gel. Roll two dark brown fondant ovals for the horse's eyes. Attach with piping gel.

## More to Know

*Strip cutters are handy for quick and easy decorating. They are used for the bridle on the horse cookies as well as the band on the cowboy hat.*

★★

# COWBOY HAT CAKE POPS

## You Will Need

rolled fondant in white and color of choice

flower former

2¾" (7 cm) circle cutter

dipping fork

chocolate candy coating in white, pink, or butterscotch

5 mm strip cutter

flower plunger

candy bead

powdered sugar

## Techniques

Cake Balls, page 53

Rolled Fondant Basics, page 28

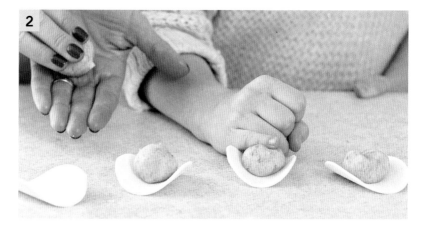

1. At least one day ahead of time, make the brim for the cowboy hat. Dust the work surface with powdered sugar. Roll kneaded and softened white rolled fondant thin. Cut the rolled fondant using a round cutter. Place the round cut shape in a U-shaped flower former. Allow the brim to harden at least 24 hours.

2. Mix up a batch of cake balls, following instruction on page 53. Roll the cake pop in a ball. Place the ball on the hardened brim. Use your index finger to indent the top of the ball.

*Sandwich cookies dipped in butterscotch chocolate coating are adorned using a chocolate transfer sheet printed with a pink floral pattern (page 50).*

**3.** Melt the candy coating. Set the cake pop on a dipping fork. Rest the dipping fork on the side of the bowl. Spoon melted pink, white, or butterscotch coating onto the cake pop. Tap the dipping fork to allow excess chocolate to fall from the brim. Slide the dipped hat on a sheet of parchment to set. Allow to set completely.

**4.** Roll kneaded and softened colored rolled fondant thin. Cut the fondant using a strip cutter. Lift one strip and wrap it around the cowboy hat. Attach with piping gel.

**5.** Dust the work surface with powdered sugar. Roll kneaded and softened white rolled fondant thin. Firmly press a flower plunger cutter into the rolled fondant, holding the base of the cutter—do not hold on to the plunger when cutting. Lift the cutter and gently run your finger along the edge of the cutter to ensure the cut is clean. Push the trigger to release the cut flower. Attach the flower to the cowboy hat with piping gel. Add a dot of piping gel in the center of the flower, and attach a candy bead for the flower center.

# Tropical Luau

★

## SAND BUCKET CUPCAKES

### You Will Need

jumbo cupcake pan

3" (7.6 cm) plastic sand buckets

buttercream icing, ivory

1 cup (200 g) sanding sugar

1 cup (230 g) brown sugar

tip #1A

crab sucker mold

chocolate coating, pink

sucker sticks

shell candy mold

⅛ pound (56.7 g) milk chocolate coating

½ pound (226.8 g) white chocolate coating

small brush

squeeze bottle

pearl dusting powder

soft brush for dusting

### Techniques

Baking Cupcakes, page 24

Icing Cupcakes, page 33

Buttercream Basics, page 28

Coordinating Party Treats, page 48

1. Make the crab suckers following instructions for molding suckers on page 49. Melt milk chocolate coating. Brush a very thin layer of milk chocolate coating in the shell candy mold. The brush strokes should be visible, and light should be showing through when the mold is held up to a light. Allow to set at room temperature.

2. Melt white chocolate and pour it into a squeeze bottle. Fill the shell candy mold. Place the filled mold in the freezer to set. Check the mold after 5 minutes. The shells should fall from the mold. If not, return to the freezer for a few more minutes.

3. Remove the shells from the freezer and place on a sheet of parchment. Allow the shells to warm to room temperature. Using a brush with soft bristles, brush the shells with pearl dust.

### More to Know

*Jumbo cupcakes are baked to fit into a mini-size sand bucket. Look for these sand buckets at party supply stores or online.*

# SAND BUCKET CUPCAKES *(continued)*

**4.** Bake and cool jumbo cupcakes. Peel off the baking cup paper. Drop the baked cupcake in the plastic bucket. Gently press the cupcake so that it fills the bottom half of the bucket.

**5.** In a mixing bowl, combine the brown sugar and sanding sugar. Fit a pastry bag with tip #1A. Fill the bag with ivory buttercream. Pipe icing onto the top of the cupcake. Sprinkle the top with the brown sugar/sanding sugar mixture.

**6.** Insert the crab sucker and add the shells.

## Younger Kids

*Younger kids can brush piping gel on the cookie and place the rolled fondant piece on top. The hearts, flowers, and stars placed on the cookies are easy for little kids to cut and plunge. Younger children have plenty to do when assisting with these cupcakes. They can sprinkle the brown sugar/sanding sugar mixture onto the iced cupcakes and then place on the crab and arrange the seashells.*

# SUNGLASSES AND FLIP-FLOP COOKIES

## You Will Need

flip-flop cookie cutter

sunglasses cookie cutter

piping gel

powdered sugar

rolled fondant in hot pink, purple, yellow, orange, green, blue, and black

plunger cutters, such as small heart, star, or flower

6 mm strip cutter

## Techniques

Rolling and Baking Cookies, page 44

Icing cookies, page 46

Rolled Fondant Basics, page 28

1. Bake cookies following instructions on page 44. For the flip-flops, if only one cookie cutter is used (and not a pair), flip over half of the flip-flops before baking to obtain a right and left flip-flop. Allow the cookies to cool completely. Using a pastry brush, brush a very thin layer of piping gel on the cookies. Dust the work surface with powdered sugar. Roll kneaded and softened rolled fondant thin. Cut the fondant with the same cutter used in baking. Place the cut fondant on the piping gel-coated cookie. Flip over the fondant and cut the other flip-flop. Flip the fondant piece back over and place the cut fondant on the other piping gel-coated cookie.

2. To decorate the flip-flops, prepare fondant as above. Firmly press one of the plunger cutters into the rolled fondant, holding the base of the cutter. Lift the cutter and gently run your finger along the edge of the cutter to ensure the cut is clean. Push the trigger to release the cut shape. Add dots of piping gel on the flip-flops. Place the cut shapes on the flip-flops and gently press.

3. For the straps, roll kneaded and softened rolled fondant thin. Cut the fondant using a strip cutter. Attach the strips with piping gel.

4. For the sunglasses cookies, apply black rolled fondant as in step 1. Brush a small amount of piping gel around the edges of the fondant on the cookie. Prepare and cut a bright color of rolled fondant. Using a paring knife, cut out the lens of the glasses. Place on the black fondant-covered cookie. Add accents using plunger cutters following step 2 above.

# Age of the Dinosaurs

★★

## DINOSAUR CAKE

### You Will Need

8" (20.3 cm) cake pan

piping gel

buttercream icing, light blue

crushed chocolate sandwich cookie crumbs

rolled fondant in red, electric green, blue, and orange

1" (2.5 cm) round cookie cutter

1½" (3.8 cm) round cookie cutter

black nonpareils

small flower cookie cutter

flower former

powdered sugar

### Techniques

Baking Cakes, page 20

Icing Cakes, page 32

Buttercream and Rolled Fondant Basics, page 28

1. At least one day ahead of time, mold the fondant dinosaurs. The blue and orange dinosaurs were formed the same way. The orange has a longer neck. To shape the two dinosaurs, first make the legs. Knead and soften the rolled fondant. Roll a snake. Cut four equal parts.

2. Set the legs up and stand in position. Roll a cone shape for the body.

### Important

*The hand-molded dinosaurs may collapse if the rolled fondant is too soft. For best results, knead in 1 tablespoon of tylose to 1 pound of rolled fondant. Tylose will make the dinosaurs more stable and less likely to collapse. Allow the rolled fondant to set for 24 hours before forming the dinosaurs. The green dinosaur's scalloped head should be made at least 24 hours before placing the head on the body.*

**3.** Gently pinch about ⅓ down from the larger (rounded) end.

**4.** Roll the upper portion of the pinched end between your palms to form a neck. The orange dinosaur's neck is slightly longer, so roll it until the neck is the desired length.

**5.** Brush piping gel on the top of the legs. Place the dinosaur's body on the legs. Add a tiny dot of piping gel to mark the eye placement. Add two black nonpareils for the eyes. Roll various sizes of small balls and flatten for the spots. Attach the spots with piping gel.

**6.** For the spikes on the blue dinosaur, knead and soften the rolled fondant. Form a cone. Flatten the cone. Cut the rounded part off so that spike is a triangle shape. Attach to the dinosaur's back with piping gel.

**7.** At least a day ahead of time, make the scalloped shape for the green dinosaur's head. Roll kneaded and

softened green rolled fondant thin. Cut a flower shape for the head. Cut off the bottom petals. Place the flower in a flower former (see page 58) and allow it to harden overnight. To make the green dinosaur, repeat steps 1 and 2 above. Place the dinosaur body on the legs, attaching with piping gel. Roll 2 small cones from white rolled fondant for the horns. Roll an egg shape for the face. Attach the face to the shaped flower using piping gel. Add a tiny dot of piping gel to mark the eye placement. Add two black nonpareils for the eyes. Attach the horns with piping gel.

**8.** Bake a two-layer 8" (20.3 cm) round cake, following instructions on page 20. Ice the cake with light blue buttercream, following instructions on page 32. Sprinkle the top with cookie crumbs.

**9.** Dust the work surface with powdered sugar. Roll different colors of kneaded and softened rolled fondant thin. Cut into circles. Attach to the side of the cake with piping gel.

## Younger Kids

*Allow your young helpers to sprinkle the crushed cookies onto the cake. They can also cut the rolled fondant circles for the cake. After the circles are cut, pipe a dot of piping gel on the cake and allow them to set the cut circles in place. They can also dip the tops of the cupcakes into the crushed cookies and arrange the candy dinosaurs and candy rocks.*

# DINOSAUR CUPCAKES

## You Will Need

standard cupcake pan

dinosaur silicone candy mold

crushed chocolate sandwich cookie crumbs

chocolate buttercream icing

chocolate coating in red, blue, green, and orange

tip #1A

chocolate rocks

## Techniques

Baking cupcakes, page 24

Icing cupcakes, page 33

Coordinating Party Treats, page 48

Buttercream Basics, page 28

1. Bake and cool the cupcakes. With melted candy coating, paint the details in the dinosaur molds following directions on page 49. Allow the details to set at room temperature. When set, fill the cavity with a contrasting color of melted chocolate coating. Place the mold in the freezer for approximately 5 minutes to set. The dinosaurs should fall from the mold. If not, return mold to the freezer for a few more minutes.

2. Fit a pastry bag with tip #1A. Fill the bag with chocolate buttercream. Pipe the icing onto the cupcake. Dip the iced cupcake in cookie crumbs. Arrange the chocolate dinosaurs with chocolate rocks.

## More to Know

*The egg cake pops and dinosaur suckers are arranged in rectangular containers with Styrofoam underneath. Artificial wheatgrass is placed on top of the Styrofoam and the sticks are stuck through the grass and into the Styrofoam.*

# DINOSAUR EGG CAKE POPS

★★

**You Will Need**

chocolate coating, white

rolled fondant in red, electric green, blue, and orange

piping gel

sucker sticks

**Technique**

Cake Balls, page 53

**1.** Mix up a batch of egg-shaped cake balls dipped in white chocolate coating following instructions on page 53.

**2.** Knead and soften the rolled fondant. Roll the fondant in various sizes of balls. Flatten the balls. Place the flatten circles on the cake pop, attaching with piping gel.

## Coordinating Treats

*Dinosaur candy suckers are painted with blue, green, orange, and red candy coating (instructions page 49). The flat eggs on the cake stand are made by piping dots on a plain egg candy mold with blue, green, orange, and red candy coating. After the dots set up at room temperature, a squeeze bottle is used to fill the egg candy mold with white chocolate candy coating.*

# Magical Princess

★★

## PRINCESS CAKE

**You Will Need**

doll dress cake form

doll cake pick

buttercream icing, white

rolled fondant, pink

2" (5.1 cm) heart cookie cutter

premade icing flowers, pink

piping gel

powdered sugar

**Techniques**

Baking Cakes, page 30

Icing cakes, page 32

Buttercream and Rolled Fondant Basics, page 28

1. Bake a cake using a doll form cake pan, following instructions for baking a cake on page 20. Ice the cake with white buttercream, following instructions on page 32. Place the cake on a cake stand. Insert a doll cake pick into the top of the iced cake. Brush her bodice and back with piping gel.

## More to Know

*Use a special domed-shape doll dress pan to make the doll dress. You will also need a doll pick—a doll with only a head and bodice and a long pick from the waist down.*

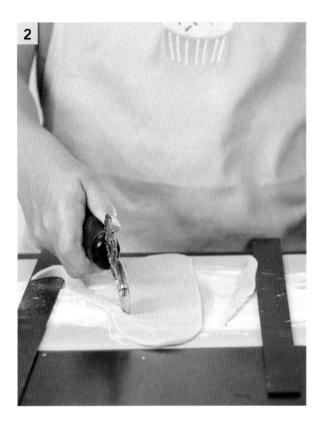

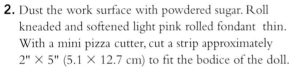

**2.** Dust the work surface with powdered sugar. Roll kneaded and softened light pink rolled fondant thin. With a mini pizza cutter, cut a strip approximately 2" × 5" (5.1 × 12.7 cm) to fit the bodice of the doll.

**3.** Wrap the fondant strip around the doll. Press gently to attach. Cut off excess in the center of the doll's back. Press the seam together.

**4.** If the icing on the skirt has crusted, use a pastry brush and brush a stripe of piping gel along the bottom of the skirt.

**5.** Dust the work surface with powdered sugar. Roll kneaded and softened light pink rolled fondant thin. Cut out several hearts using the cookie cutter.

**6.** Place the hearts upside-down in a row around the bottom of the cake. Slightly overlap the hearts.

**7.** Brush another piping gel strip just above the first row of hearts. Start a second row of hearts just above the first row. The hearts should conceal the white icing underneath. If the icing is showing, place the hearts a little lower.

**8.** Continue adding fondant hearts in rows until the skirt is covered. Add a dot of piping gel to attach the icing flowers around the doll's waist.

4

5

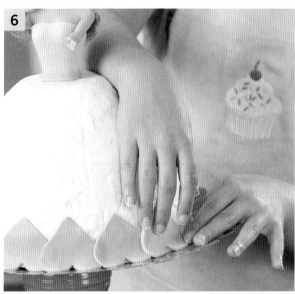

6

7

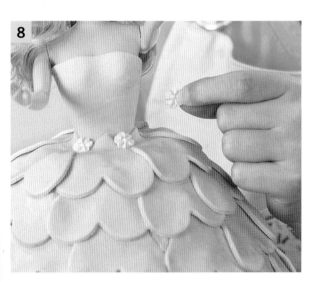

8

## Coordinating Treats

Heart cookies (page 44) are covered with a candy coating (page 46) and then sprinkled with sugar to add a touch of sparkle.

# STAR WANDS

## You Will Need

sheet of crispy rice cereal treat (or follow the recipe below)

chocolate candy coating

sanding sugar

sucker stick or straw

star cookie cutter

## Technique

Coordinating Party Treats, page 48

## Crispy Rice Cereal Treats Recipe

3 tablespoons (42 g) butter

4 cups (960 mL) miniature marshmallows

6 cups (1.4 L) crispy rice cereal

In a microwave-safe bowl heat butter and marshmallows on HIGH for 3 minutes, stirring after 2 minutes. Stir until smooth. Add the crispy rice cereal and spread the mixture into a buttered 9" × 13" (22.9 × 33 cm) pan. Microwave cooking times may vary.

1. Mix up a batch or buy a commercially prepared large sheet of crispy rice cereal treats. Allow the recipe to set completely. Using a cookie cutter, cut out a star shape.

2. Press the treat in the center to release the cut star from the cookie cutter. If the star is sticking, spray the cookie cutter with a grease cooking spray before cutting additional stars.

3. Melt the chocolate candy coating. Hold on to the star and dip the top in the melted candy coating.

4. Place the dipped star on a sheet of parchment. Sprinkle with sanding sugar before the chocolate coating sets.

5. Allow the star to set completely. When the chocolate coating has set, insert a straw (shown) or a sucker stick into the bottom of the cut star.

## Younger Kids

*Young children love sprinkles! Let them sprinkle sugars onto the heart cookies and star wands. Little ones can also assist in cutting the rolled fondant hearts for the cake.*

# Festive Party Cake and Treats

★ ★ ★

## PRESENT CAKE

### You Will Need

8" (20.3 cm) square cake pan

mini pizza cutter

1" (2.5 cm) round cutter

piping gel

rolled fondant in red, pink, green, lime green, light blue, and white

buttercream icing

powdered sugar

### Techniques

Baking Cakes, page 20

Covering cakes with rolled fondant, page 34

Cake boards and Cake stands, page 36

Rolled Fondant Basics, page 28

**1.** At least one day ahead of time, make the loops for the top of the cake. Dust the work surface with powdered sugar. Roll kneaded and softened rolled fondant thin. Using a mini pizza cutter, cut a 1" × 6" (2.5 × 15.2 cm) strip of rolled fondant.

**2.** Brush the end of the cut strip with piping gel.

## Important

*You must make the bow loops for the top of the cake and the curly streamers for the cupcakes at least a day ahead so they can harden. You can also make the dots at this time if you choose, although this is not necessary.*

## More to Know

*This cake also looks great when iced with buttercream instead of covered with rolled fondant.*

# PRESENT CAKE *(continued)*

**3.** Fold the strip in half, being careful that the loop remains. Pinch the flat ends together and stand the loop on its side. For a full bow, make about 25 loops. Allow the loops to harden overnight before assembling the bow on the cake. If the bow loops are collapsing while being placed on their side, the fondant is not stiff enough. Tylose, a product available at cake decorating supply stores, can be added to the rolled fondant to stiffen it. Add approximately 1 tablespoon to 1 pound of rolled fondant.

**4.** Bake a two-layer 8" (20.3 cm) square cake, following instructions for baking on page 20. Cover the cake with white rolled fondant, following instructions on page 34. Place the cake on a cake board or a cake stand. Cut a 1" × 7" (2.5 × 17.8 cm) strip of rolled fondant for the ribbons on the side of the cake. Brush piping gel on the cake where the strip will be placed.

**5.** Attach the ribbon to the cake. Add a strip of rolled fondant on each side of the cake.

**6.** Cut various colors of rolled fondant using a small round cutter.

**7.** Attach the circles to the cake by placing a dot of piping gel on the cake where the circle will be placed. Add the circles and gently press in place.

**8.** Color buttercream icing the same color as the rolled fondant bow loops. Fill a pastry bag with the green icing. Pipe a mound of icing in the center of the cake.

**9.** Gently insert the pinched end of the loop into the icing. Arrange the loops in a circle around the icing mound.

**10.** Add layers of loops until the bow is full.

## Younger Kids

*Younger children can cut the circles for the polka dots and place them on the cake. They can also help arrange the bow loops on top of the cake. Let the little ones sprinkle the jimmies and add the streamers on the cupcakes.*

## STREAMER CUPCAKES

**You Will Need**

powdered sugar

standard cupcake pan

mini pizza cutter

dowel rod

rolled fondant in red, pink, green, lime green, and light blue

buttercream icing, white

jimmies in red, pink, green, lime green, and blue

tip #1M

**Techniques**

Baking cupcakes, page 24

Icing cupcakes, page 33

Buttercream and Rolled Fondant Basics, page 28

1. At least one day ahead of time, make the curly streamers for the cupcakes. Dust the work surface with powdered sugar. Roll kneaded and softened rolled fondant thin. Using a mini pizza cutter, cut a ¼" × 8" (6 mm × 20.3 cm) strip of rolled fondant. Wrap the cut strips around a dowel rod. Allow the streamers to harden overnight. When the streamers are hardened, gently remove from the dowel rod. The streamers can be broken into two or three pieces to create a variety of lengths.

2. Bake and cool the cupcakes. Fit a pastry bag with tip #1M. Fill the pastry bag with buttercream icing. Pipe the icing onto the cupcake.

3. Immediately add the jimmies and rolled fondant streamers.

## Coordinating Treats

*Additional treats are coordinated, such as the cake balls (page 53) and dipped pretzels (page 50).*

# Pirate Shindig

★★

## PIRATE SKULL AND CROSS BONES CAKE

### You Will Need

8" (20.3 cm) round cake pan

skull cookie cutter

bone cookie cutters

food color marker, black

mini pizza cutter

chocolate gold coins

buttercream icing, white

rolled fondant in white, sky blue, red, and dark ivory

piping gel

powdered sugar

1 cup (230 g) brown sugar

1 cup (200 g) white sanding sugar

### Techniques

Baking Cakes, page 20

Icing cakes, page 32

Cake boards and Cake stands, page 36

Buttercream and Rolled Fondant Basics, page 28

1. At least a day ahead of time, roll kneaded and softened white rolled fondant thin. Cut out 4 bones and the skull with cookie cutters. Cut off one end of each bone with the skull cutter so the bones will fit around the skull like a puzzle. Allow to harden overnight.

2. Bake a two-layer 8" (20.3 cm) round cake, following instructions on page 20. Ice the cakes with white buttercream, following instructions on page 32. Dust the work surface with powdered sugar. Roll kneaded and softened sky blue rolled fondant thin. With a mini pizza cutter, cut an 8" (20.3 cm) circle using the 8" (20.3 cm) cake pan as a guide. Place the fondant circle on top of the iced cake.

3. Roll kneaded and softened red rolled fondant thin. With a mini pizza cutter, cut 1" (2.5 cm) wide strips that are the same height as the cake. Place the strips around the side of the cake. If the icing has crusted, brush a bit of piping gel on the back of the strip to adhere.

4. Draw the details on the skull using a black food color marker.

5. Place the skull and bones on top of the cake using piping gel to adhere.

6. Mix together 1 cup of brown sugar and 1 cup of white sanding sugar. Cover a 12" (30.5) cake board with dark ivory rolled fondant, following instructions on page 37.

7. Brush the board with piping gel.

## Important

*Make the skull on the cake, skull on the pirate hat cookies, shark fins on the cupcakes, and maps for the cupcakes at least a day ahead to allow time for the rolled fondant to harden.*

8. Sprinkle the board with the mixture of sugars. Pat gently.

9. Lift the cake and gently place on the cake board. Arrange chocolate coins covered with gold foil around the cake.

# PIRATE CUPCAKES

## You Will Need

standard cupcake pan

buttercream icing in ivory and sky blue

rolled fondant in ivory and electric blue

1 cup (230 g) brown sugar

1 cup (200 g) white sanding sugar

food color markers

piping gel

## Techniques

Baking cupcakes, page 24

Icing cupcakes, page 33

Buttercream and Rolled Fondant Basics, page 28

1. At least a several hours or a day ahead of time, roll kneaded and softened dark ivory rolled fondant thin. Tear small rectangle shapes to resemble a torn pirate map. Roll corners of the map. Allow to harden.

2. After the maps have hardened, draw the details on the map using food color markers.

3. At least several hours or a day ahead of time, knead and soften the sky blue rolled fondant. Roll the fondant into a ball; then form into a cone by wedging the ball between your palms and rolling.

4. Flatten the cone and curve the pointed end to resemble a shark fin.

5. Mix together the brown sugar and white sanding sugar. Ice half of the cupcakes with ivory buttercream. Dip the iced cupcakes in the sugar mixture. Add the map, adhering with a dot of piping gel.

6. Ice the other half of the cupcakes with sky blue buttercream. Allow the buttercream to crust (30–45 minutes). Brush the iced cupcakes with a thin layer of piping gel. Insert the sharks fin into the iced cupcake.

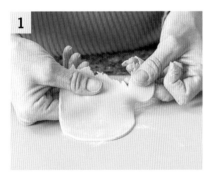

★ ★

# PIRATE COOKIES

### You Will Need

pirate hat cookie cutter

shark cookie cutter

powdered sugar

rolled fondant in black, white, red, and sky blue

round plunger cutter

nonpareils, black

piping gel

food color marker, black

### Techniques

Rolling and Baking Cookies, page 44

Rolled Fondant Basics, page 28

Icing Cookies, page 46

1. Bake and cool cookies, following instructions on page 44. Using a pastry brush, brush a very thin layer of piping gel on the cookie. Dust the work surface with powdered sugar. Roll knead and softened rolled fondant thin. Cut the fondant with the same cutter used in baking. Place the cut fondant on the piping gel-coated cookie. For the polka dots, roll kneaded and softened rolled fondant very thin. Hold on to the base of the plunger cutter to cut the circles. Lift the plunger and push the trigger to release the circles. Add a dot of piping gel to attach the circles to the cookie.

2. At least one day ahead of time, make the skulls. Roll the white fondant into a cone shape. Press the cone shape to flatten into a skull form. Attach the skull to the pirate hat using piping gel to adhere. Allow the skull to harden several hours. Draw the details on the hat's skull using a black food color marker. Place a black nonpareil on the shark for his eye, using a very small dot of piping gel to adhere.

## Younger Kids

*Little hands can help decorate the cookies by placing on the cut fondant shapes. Children can also help dip the cupcake tops into the sugar mixture. They can add the maps and the shark fins to the cupcakes. Ask children to sprinkle the sugar mixture onto the cake board and scatter the gold coins.*

# Jungle Jamboree

★★

## JUNGLE CAKE

### You Will Need

8" (20.3 cm) round cake pan

rolled fondant in light green, green, light brown, brown, yellow, orange, white, blue, light blue, and light orange

nonpareils, black

leaf cutter

palm tree cutter

jungle cutie cupcake cutters

1" (2.5 cm) round circle cutter

mini accent cutter set

extruder

piping gel

### Techniques

Baking Cakes, page 20

Covering Cakes with Rolled Fondant, page 34

Rolled Fondant Basics, page 28

**1.** Bake and cool an 8" (20.3 cm) round cake, following instructions on page 20. Cover the cake with light green rolled fondant (page 34). Roll kneaded and softened brown rolled fondant thin. Cut out the trunk. Place the trunk on the cake, attaching with piping gel. Roll kneaded and softened green rolled fondant thin. Cut out the palms. Place the palms on the cake, attaching with piping gel.

## Important

*Make the jungle animals at least 24 hours ahead of time if placing them on the cupcakes. If you are using the animals on the cake or cookies, you do not have to make them ahead of time, though doing so will make it easier to arrange them animals on the cake and cookies.*

**2.** Make jungle animals following steps 1–7 on pages 112–113. Roll kneaded and softened green rolled fondant thin. Cut out several leaves. Cut some of the leaves in half, some in thirds, and leave some as they are. Arrange the leaves and the animals on the cake, attaching with piping gel.

**3.** Fit the extruder with a disk that has a single round opening. Roll kneaded and softened green rolled fondant into a snake. Feed the extruder with the rolled fondant. Extrude the fondant, creating a vine. Attach to the cake with piping gel.

# JUNGLE CUPCAKES

### You Will Need

standard cupcake pan

buttercream icing, electric green

tip #1M

rolled fondant, light brown, brown, yellow, orange, white, blue, light blue, and light orange

nonpareils, black

jungle cutie cupcake cutters

1" (2.5 cm) round circle cutter

mini accent cutter set

piping gel

### Techniques

Baking Cupcakes, page 24

Icing Cupcakes, page 33

Rolled Fondant Basics, page 28

**1.** Bake and cool cupcakes, following instructions on page 24.

**2.** At least a day ahead of time, make the jungle animals, following steps 1–7 on pages 112–113.

**3.** Fit a pastry bag with tip #1M. Fill the bag with electric green buttercream. Pipe the icing on the cupcake. Place the jungle animals on the icing.

# JUNGLE COOKIES

**You Will Need**

3½" (8.9 cm) scalloped square cutter

jungle cutie cupcake cutters

1" (2.5 cm) round circle cutter

mini accent cutter set

rolled fondant in light green, light brown, brown, yellow, orange, white, blue, light blue, and light orange

nonpareils, black

piping gel

**Techniques**

Rolling and Baking Cookies, page 44

Icing cookies, page 46

Rolled Fondant Basics, page 28

1

1. Make the jungle animals. To make the giraffe, roll kneaded and softened yellow rolled fondant thin. Cut out the giraffe. Roll kneaded and softened orange rolled fondant into several sizes of tiny balls. Press and flatten the orange balls. Attach to the giraffe with piping gel.

2. Roll kneaded and softened white rolled fondant thin. Cut out a small oval. Using piping gel, attach the oval for the giraffe's nose. Use a toothpick to add the nostrils. Roll two small cones with kneaded and softened light brown rolled fondant. Attach to the giraffe's horns with piping gel.

3. Use a small brush and piping gel to make two small eyes. Set black nonpareils on the piping gel eyes.

4. To make the lion, roll kneaded and softened light orange rolled fondant thin. Cut out the lion. Roll kneaded and softened orange rolled fondant thin. Using the lion cutter, cut out a second lion. Cut off the body from the mane using the scalloped edge of a mini pizza cutter. Attach the mane to the lion's body using piping gel.

5. Roll kneaded and softened light orange rolled fondant thin. Cut out the lion's head using a 1" (2.5 cm) round circle cutter. Cut a tiny circle using a round cutter from a mini accent cutter set. Cut the circle in half for the lion's ears. Knead and soften the orange rolled fondant. Roll a small cone for the lion's tail. Attach the ears, head, and tail with piping gel.

6. Roll kneaded and softened white rolled fondant thin. Cut out a small circle using the 1" (2.5 cm) round cutter. With the same round cutter, cut the upper third of the circle, creating a football shape. Attach the football shape to the lion's face for his nose and cheeks. Run a paring knife down the middle of the cut football shape to emboss a line for his

mouth. Attach to the lion with piping gel. Add black nonpareils for the lion's eyes, using piping gel to attach. The elephant and monkey are made like the giraffe and the lion. The elephant is made with light blue rolled fondant. His ear is made with a paisley shape cutter from the mini accent cutter set. The monkey is made with brown rolled fondant. His nose is made using an oval cutter from the mini accent cutter set.

**7.** Bake and cool square scalloped cookies using the 3½" (8.9 cm) cutter. Roll kneaded and softened light green rolled fondant thin. Cut the fondant using the same cutter used in baking. Attach the fondant to the cookies with piping gel. Place a dot of piping gel in the center of the fondant-covered cookie. Place a jungle animal in the center.

# Owl Hootenanny

★★★

## OWL CAKE

### You Will Need

14" × 11" (35.6 × 27.9 cm) oval cake pan

powdered sugar

rolled fondant in electric green, pink, white, orange, turquoise, light brown, and dark brown

food color marker

2¼" (5.7 cm) round cookie cutter

1" (2.5 cm) round cookie cutter

3½" (8.9 cm) flower cookie cutter

mini pizza cutter

buttercream icing

piping gel

3½" (8.9 cm) diamond cutter

### Techniques

Baking Cakes, page 20

Covering Cakes with Rolled Fondant, page 34

Rolled Fondant Basics, page 28

1. At least one day ahead of time, make the owl's wings following the pattern on page 117. Dust the work surface with powdered sugar. Roll kneaded and softened electric green rolled fondant thin. Use a mini pizza cutter to cut around the pattern.

2. Bake and cool the oval-shaped cake. This size of cake will take about 1½ cake mixes to get a 2" (5.1 cm) tall cake. Position the oval pan used in baking on the upper quarter of the cake. Using a food color marker, trace around the pan to form the owl ears. Use a serrated knife to trim off the top quarter of the owl, using the food color marker line as the guide.

## Important

*Make the owl's wings for the cake, and the owls for the cupcakes, at least 24 hours ahead of time.*

## More to Know

*The owl suckers are arranged in a small basket lined with plastic wrap. The lined basket is filled ¾ full with candy clay (page 52), which is used as a filler and as a place to hold the sucker sticks in the pot.*

# OWL CAKE *(continued)*

**3.** Ice the cake, following instructions on page 32.

**4.** Transfer the cake to a cake board. Cover the cake with the light brown rolled fondant, following instructions on page 34. Dust the work surface with powdered sugar. Roll kneaded and softened turquoise rolled fondant thin. Use a ruler to cut a straight strip for the owl's stripes.

**5.** Attach to the cake with piping gel. Add a total of 3 stripes.

**6.** Knead and soften the white rolled fondant. Dust the work surface with powdered sugar. Cut two eyes using a 2¼" (5.7 cm) round cookie cutter. Knead and soften the pink rolled fondant. Dust the work surface with powdered sugar. Cut 2 flowers using a cookie cutter. Knead and soften the dark brown rolled fondant. Dust the work surface with powdered sugar. Cut two pupils using a 1" (2.5 cm) round cookie cutter. Layer the eyes using piping gel to adhere. Attach the eyes to the cake using piping gel.

**7.** Knead and soften the orange rolled fondant. Dust the work surface with powdered sugar. Cut a diamond. Cut the diamond in half. Use one-half of the diamond for the beak.

**8.** Attach the wings to the cake using piping gel.

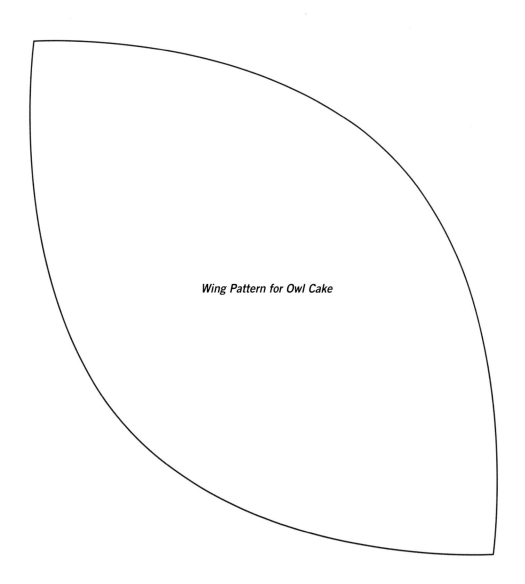

*Wing Pattern for Owl Cake*

## OWL CUPCAKES

**You Will Need**

standard cupcake pan

powdered sugar

buttercream icing, light pink

rolled fondant in electric green, pink, white, orange, turquoise, light brown, and dark brown

tiny triangle cutter

tiny round cutter

tiny wing cutter

5 mm strip cutter

flower plunger cutter

owl cutie cupcake cutter

food color marker, black

piping gel

tip #1M

**Techniques**

Baking Cupcakes, page 24

Icing Cupcakes, page 33

Buttercream and Rolled Fondant Basics, page 28

**1.** At least several hours or one day ahead of time, make rolled fondant owls. Dust the work surface with powdered sugar. Roll kneaded and softened light brown fondant thin. Cut the owls using the owl cupcake cutter. Dust the work surface with additional powdered sugar, if needed. Roll knead and softened bright colors of rolled fondant thin. Using a flower plunger cutter for the eyes, firmly press into the rolled fondant, holding the base of the cutter. Do not hold on to the plunger when cutting. Lift the cutter and gently run your finger along the edge of the cutter to ensure the cut is clean. Push the trigger to release the cut flower. If the cut flower remains on the work surface, use a spatula with a thin blade to remove the flower. Dust the surface with additional powdered sugar before cutting more flowers. Use a mini round cutter for the center of the flower and for spots on the owls. Use the mini wing cutter for the wings. Cut stripes for the owls using a strip cutter. Attach all of the pieces using piping gel. After several hours, draw a dot using a black food color marker on the eye.

**2.** Fit a pastry bag with tip #1M. Fill the bag with light pink buttercream. Pipe a swirl on the cupcake.

**3.** Place the fondant owls on the cupcake.

### Younger Kids

*Small fingers are sized just right to add the tiny details onto the cut owls used for these cookies and cupcakes. The little ones can also help decorate the cookies by brushing on piping gel and placing the cut fondant scalloped circles in place. Pipe a dot of piping gel in the center of the cookie and allow younger kids to set the decorated owl in place.*

### ★★★

# OWL COOKIES

## You Will Need

rolled fondant, electric green, pink, white, orange, turquoise, light brown, and dark brown

powdered sugar

piping gel

mini triangle cutter

mini round cutter

mini wing cutter

5 mm strip cutter

flower plunger cutter

buttercream icing

owl cutie cupcake cutter

food color marker, black

3½" (8.9 cm) round cookie cutter

3¼" (8.3 cm) fluted round cookie cutter

## Techniques

Rolling and Baking Cookies, page 44

Icing Cookies, page 46

Rolled Fondant Basics, page 28

1. Follow step 1 on opposite page for making the owls.

2. Bake and cool cookies using a round cookie cutter.

3. Dust the work surface with powdered sugar. Roll kneaded and softened rolled fondant thin; cut the fondant using a fluted round cutter. Brush the cookie with a thin layer of piping gel. Place the piece on top of the piping gel-covered cookie.

4. Brush a dime-size circle of piping gel in the center of the fondant-covered cookie. Place the layered owl in the center.

*Coordinating Treats*

*Owl candy suckers are painted with blue, green, pink, white, and orange candy coating. After the details are painted, they are filled with milk chocolate candy coating (page 49).*

# Construction Zone

★ ★

## CONSTRUCTION CAKE

### You Will Need

12" × 18" (30.5 × 45.7 cm) cake pan

number pan

chocolate buttercream icing

tip#1A

tip #21

crushed chocolate sandwich cookie crumbs

plastic construction vehicles

chocolate rocks

rolled fondant in white and black

powdered sugar

5 mm strip cutter

piping gel

### Techniques

Baking Cakes, page 20

Icing Cakes, page 32

Cake Boards and Cake Stands, page 36

Buttercream and Rolled Fondant Basics, page 28

1. Bake and cool a cake using a number pan. Cover the cake with black rolled fondant, following instructions on page 34. Bake and cool a 12" × 18" (30.5 × 45.7 cm) sheet cake. Ice the cake with chocolate buttercream, following instructions on page 32. Place the rolled fondant-covered number on the sheet cake. Fit a pastry bag with tip #1A. Fill the bag with chocolate buttercream. Pipe mounds of chocolate buttercream. Spoon crushed cookie crumbs all over the cake, gently pressing to attach to the icing.

2. Dust the work surface with powdered sugar. Knead and soften the white rolled fondant and roll it thin. Use a strip cutter to cut strips of fondant. Cut apart the strips using a paring knife.

3. Arrange the cut strips on the number cake. Attach with piping gel. Arrange the construction vehicles and chocolate rocks on the cake. Fit a pastry bag with tip #21. Fill the bag with chocolate buttercream. Pipe a star border.

## More to Know

*A small number pan is used for the top of the cake. These pans take less than one cake mix. The number pans are part of a Pantastic line, a line of pans made of a plastic that can be used in the oven.*

# CONSTRUCTION HAT AND ORANGE CONE CUPCAKES

**You Will Need**

standard cupcake pan

construction hat candy mold

yellow chocolate coating

candy color, orange and yellow

squeeze bottle

orange candy coating

square crackers

candy dipping tool

chocolate buttercream icing

tip #1A

crushed chocolate sandwich cookie crumbs

**Techniques**

Baking Cupcakes, page 24

Icing Cupcakes, page 33

Coordinating Party Treats, page 48

Cake Balls, page 53

Buttercream Basics, page 28

1. Melt yellow chocolate coating. Add yellow candy color and a touch of orange candy color to obtain a gold chocolate coating. Pour the melted gold coating in a squeeze bottle. Fill the cavities of the construction hat mold. Place the filled mold in the freezer to set. Check the mold after 15 minutes. The hats should fall from the mold. If not, return them to the freezer for a few more minutes.

2. Mix up a batch of cake balls, following instruction on page 53. Roll the cake in a ball, then in a cone. Place the shaped cone on top of a square cracker.

3. Melt orange candy coating. Set the cake cone and cracker on a dipping fork. Rest the dipping fork on the side of the bowl. Spoon melted coating onto the cake cone and cracker. Tap the dipping fork on the bowl to allow excess chocolate to fall from the cone. Slide the dipped cone on a sheet of parchment to set. Allow to set completely.

4. Fit a pastry bag with tip #1A. Fill the bag with chocolate buttercream. Pipe chocolate buttercream on top of the cupcake. Dip the top of the cupcake in the cookie crumbs. Place the hat or cone on top of the cupcake.

# CONSTRUCTION TOOL COOKIES

**You Will Need**

tool cookie cutters

powdered sugar

rolled fondant in gray, red, orange, blue, and green

tiny circle cutter

super pearl dust

piping gel

**Techniques**

Rolling and Baking Cookies, page 44

Icing Cookies, page 46

Rolled Fondant Basics, page 28

1. Bake and cool cookies, following instructions on page 44. Using a pastry brush, brush a very thin layer of piping gel on the cookie. Dust the work surface with powdered sugar. Roll kneaded and softened gray rolled fondant thin. Cut the fondant with the same cutter used in baking.

2. Some tools will have a contrasting color of handle; cut the gray fondant where the contrasting piece will be placed. Place the cut fondant on the piping gel coated cookie.

3. Cut a small circle of gray fondant to represent a screw on the pliers. Attach the small circle using a dot of piping gel. Brush the gray fondant with super pearl dust. Roll red, orange, blue, or green fondant the same thickness as the gray piece on the cookie. Cut with the same cutter used in baking. Cut the handle off and place on the cookie.

## Younger Kids

*Young children can dip the cupcake tops into the crushed cookies and then place the hat or cone on the top. Let little ones help with the cake by sprinkling the crushed cookies all over the cake and arranging the trucks and candy rocks. Younger kids can also help decorate the cookies by placing on the cut fondant shapes and brushing the cookies with the pearl dust.*

# Puppy Valentine

★ ★ ★

## PUPPY VALENTINE CUPCAKES

### You Will Need

standard cupcake pan

buttercream icing in white and black

rolled fondant in brown, white, red, and pink

powdered sugar

tip #2

2¾" (7 cm) heart cookie cutter

3¼" (8.3 cm) heart cookie cutter

¾" (1.9 cm) circle cutter

tiny teardrop cutter

heart icing layons, red (available premade at cake supply stores)

### Techniques

Baking Cupcakes, page 24

Icing Cupcakes, page 33

Buttercream and Rolled Fondant Basics, page 28

1. At least several hours or one day ahead of time, make the hearts and the puppy ears for the cupcakes. Dust the work surface with powdered sugar. Roll kneaded and softened brown rolled fondant thin. Cut a small heart. Cut the heart in half for the puppy ears. Roll kneaded and softened red and pink rolled fondant thin. Cut 3 large hearts. Allow the hearts and the puppy ears to harden.

2. Roll kneaded and softened pink rolled fondant thin. Cut a small circle for the puppy's spot around his eye. Use red icing hearts for the nose; if you are unable to find premade icing hearts, make the puppy nose from a red rolled fondant heart.

### Important

*Make the puppies ears and the hearts on the cupcake a day ahead of time to allow the rolled fondant to firm.*

# PUPPY VALENTINE CUPCAKES *(continued)*

## Coordinating Treats

*Chocolate suckers were made using red, pink, white, and chocolate candy coating, (page 49).*

3. Roll kneaded and softened red rolled fondant thin. Cut a tiny teardrop shape. Cut off the pointed end of the teardrop for the puppy's tongue.

4. Spread white buttercream on the cupcakes. Center the 3¼" (8.3 cm) heart on the cupcake, or decorate as a puppy face using the following instructions. Place an icing heart in the center of the cupcake for the puppy's nose. Place 1 pink circle just above and to the right of the nose for the eye patch. Gently press the puppy's ears into the side of the iced cupcake.

5. Fit a pastry bag with tip #2. Fill the bag with black buttercream. Pipe the puppy's mouth. Add the tongue. Roll two tiny brown balls for the puppy's eyes. Attach to the cupcake with piping gel.

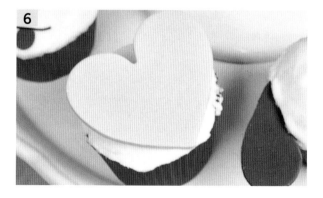

6. For the heart cupcakes, place the cut heart, made in step 1, on the iced cupcake.

# PUPPY VALENTINE COOKIES

★★

## You Will Need

puppy face cookie cutter

3¼" (8.3 cm) heart cookie cutter

piping gel

powdered sugar

rolled fondant in brown, white, red, and pink

buttercream icing, black

tip #2

¾" (1.9 cm) circle cutter

tiny teardrop cutterheart icing layons (available premade at cake supply stores)

## Techniques

Rolling and Baking Cookies, page 44

Rolled Fondant Basics, page 28

Icing Cookies, page 46

1. Bake and cool puppy face cookies, following instructions on page 44. Using a pastry brush, brush a very thin layer of piping gel on the cookie. Dust the work surface with powdered sugar. Roll kneaded and softened white rolled fondant thin. Cut the fondant with the same cutter used in baking. Cut off the ears.

2. Place the cut fondant face on the piping gel-coated cookie. Roll kneaded and softened brown rolled fondant thin. Cut the brown fondant with the puppy face cookie cutter. Cut off the ears. Place the cut ears on the piping gel-coated cookie. Add the remaining details of the puppy's face, following the same directions as for the puppy cupcakes.

3. Bake and cool heart cookies, following instructions on page 44. Using a pastry brush, brush a very thin layer of piping gel on the cookie. Dust the work surface with powdered sugar. Roll kneaded and softened red or pink rolled fondant thin. Cut the fondant with the same cutter used in baking. Place the cut heart on the piping gel-coated cookie.

## Younger Kids

*Set young children to work cutting hearts for the cupcakes as well as cutting the puppy face details.*

# Welcome Springtime

★ ★ ★

## BUNNY AND CHICK CUPCAKES

**You Will Need**

standard cupcake pan

rolled fondant in white, yellow, aqua, pink, orange, and green

tylose

angel hair pasta

buttercream icing, light green

tip #233

flower plunger cutters

food color marker, black

piping gel

powdered sugar

toothpicks

Styrofoam

foam pad and ball tool

**Techniques**

Baking Cupcakes, page 24

Piping Using Tips, page 40

Buttercream and Rolled Fondant Basics, page 28

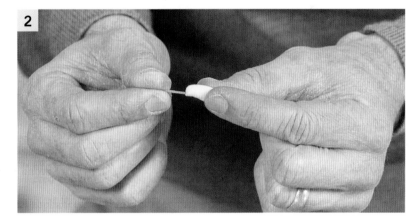

**1.** At least a day ahead of time, make the bunnies. Roll a cone for the bunny's body. Insert a toothpick through the bunny's body. Insert the bunny's body and toothpick into a piece of Styrofoam. Roll a small oval for the bunny's head. Brush a small amount of piping gel at the top of the cone. Place the head on the top of the cone and through the toothpick. Roll two small cones for the bunny's feet. Press the pointed end of the cone to flatten the back of the feet. Roll two smaller cones for the bunny's arms.

**2.** Roll two snakes for the bunny's ears. Insert a small section of angel hair pasta into each ear. Brush a dot of piping gel where the ears will be placed. Press the angel hair pasta into the bunny's head.

**3.** Brush piping gel on the flattened part of the feet. Lift the bunny's body and arrange the feet. Place the bunny on top of the flattened part of the feet. Arrange the arms on the bunny, attaching with piping gel.

**4.** Roll a cone with orange rolled fondant for the carrot. Attach the carrot to the bunny using piping gel. Roll a small cylinder for the leaf of the carrot. Attach to the carrot with piping gel. Using a black food color marker, add black dots for the bunny's eyes.

**5.** Roll an egg for the chick using yellow rolled fondant. Insert a toothpick through the chick. Insert the chick and toothpick into a piece of Styrofoam. Roll a small cone for the chick's wings. Flatten the cone. Attach the wings using piping gel.

**6.** For the beak, roll a small ball using orange rolled fondant. Squeeze the ball to form a pointy cone. Attach to the chick using a dot of piping gel. Add dots for the eyes using a black food color marker.

**7.** Dust the work surface with powdered sugar. Roll kneaded and softened aqua rolled fondant thin. Using a flower plunger cutter, firmly press into the rolled fondant, holding the base of the cutter—do not hold onto the plunger when cutting. Lift the cutter and

### Important

• Make the bunnies for the cupcakes at least a day ahead of time. For best results, knead 1 tablespoon of tylose to 1 pound of white rolled fondant. Allow the rolled fondant to set for 24 hours before forming the bunnies. Tylose will make the bunnies more stable and less likely to collapse.

• Use a toothpick to stabilize the bunnies and chicks in the cupcakes. Never cut a toothpick, as it will become a choking hazard. The bunny ears are held in place with a small section of angel hair pasta.

### Younger Kids

*It's easy for young kids to form nearly all the shapes for the hand-molded bunnies and especially the chicks. However, it may be difficult for them to assemble the bunnies. Allow little ones to add the dots for the eyes. Young kids love to watch white icing turn into pretty colors. Ask them to mix all the colors for the flower bouquet cookies. Little fingers can also gently press the icing, if there is a peak, after the flower petals are piped.*

gently run your finger along the edge of the cutter to ensure the cut is clean. Push the trigger to release the cut flower. If the flower remains on the work surface, use a spatula with a thin blade to remove the flower. Dust the surface with additional powdered sugar before cutting more flowers. Place the cut flowers on a foam pad. Cup the flowers using a ball tool. Attach the flowers to the chicks and bunnies using piping gel. Roll yellow fondant in a tiny ball for the center of the flower; attach with piping gel.

**8.** Bake and cool cupcakes. Fit a pastry bag with tip #233. Fill the bag with light green buttercream icing. Starting at the edge of the cupcake, pipe grass on the cupcake. Continue piping around the cupcake, working your way to the center until the cupcake is completely piped with grass. Insert the bunnies and chicks into the iced cupcakes.

⭐⭐

# FLOWER COOKIE BOUQUETS

## You Will Need

flower cookie cutter

leaf cookie cutter

buttercream icing in pink, yellow, blue, and light green

3 tips #2A

tip #366

candy clay

clay pot

sucker sticks

Sixlets, lime green

## Techniques

Rolling and Baking Cookies, page 44

Piping Using Tips, page 40

Buttercream Basics, page 28

1. Bake and cool flower and leaf cookies on sticks, following directions on page 44. Fit three pastry bags with tip #2A. Fill one with pink, one with blue, and one with yellow buttercream. Pipe a dot on each petal of the flower cookie. With a contrasting color, pipe a dot in the center of the flower. Allow a few minutes for the dots to crust. Use your finger to gently press and eliminate the point of the dot.

2. Fit a pastry bag with tip #366. Fill with light green buttercream. Pipe a leaf on the leaf cookie.

3. At least a day ahead of time, mix a batch of candy clay. Allow the candy clay to set for 24 hours before arranging the flowers. Line a clay pot with plastic wrap. Drop a chunk of candy clay into the lined clay pot. Seal the candy clay with the plastic wrap. Insert the cookie sticks into the candy clay, holding on to the sticks and not the cookies. Cover the candy clay with green Sixlets.

## Coordinating Treats

*Sandwich cookies dipped in light green chocolate coating are adorned using purchased bunny royal icing decorations (page 51).*

# BUNNY SUCKERS

**You Will Need**

bunny sucker mold

sucker sticks

chocolate coating in light blue, pink, yellow, and light green

squeeze bottle

candy writers in white, brown, and pink

sanding sugar, white

piping gel

**Technique**

Coordinating Party Treats, page 48

1. Paint the cavities of the bunny mold, following instructions on page 49, using white, pink, and brown candy writers. Allow the details to set.

2. Melt the candy coating and pour into a squeeze bottle. Fill the painted cavities of the bunny mold. Place the filled mold in the freezer to set. Check the mold after 10 minutes. The bunnies should fall from the mold. If not, return to the freezer for a few more minutes.

3. Brush the bunny's tail with piping gel. Sprinkle white sanding sugar on the tail.

## More to Know

- The flower cookies are arranged in a terra cotta pot lined with plastic wrap. The lined pot is filled ¾ full with candy clay (recipe page 52). The candy clay is used as a filler and as a place to hold the sticks in the pot.

- Make the candy clay for the flower cookie bouquets at least a day ahead of time to allow the candy clay to set.

# Snowy Treats

★★

## SILLY SNOWMAN CAKE

**You Will Need**

6" (15.2 cm) half ball cake pan

8" (20.3 cm) half ball cake pan

16" (40.6 cm) cake drum

buttercream icing, white

edible glitter, white

rolled fondant in blue, black, orange, blue green, red, and white

powdered sugar

2³⁄₁₆"(5.6 cm) snowflake plunger cutter

1⁹⁄₁₆" (4 cm) snowflake plunger cutter

pretzel thins

chocolate rocks, black coal

2" (5.1 cm) circle cutter

1½" (3.8 cm) circle cutter

1" (2.5 cm) circle cutter

piping gel

tip #6

**Techniques**

Baking Cakes, page 20

Icing Cakes, page 32

Cake Boards and Cake Stands, page 36

Buttercream and Rolled Fondant Basics, page 28

1. At least a day ahead of time, cover the cake drum with the sky blue rolled fondant. Set the board aside. Dust the work surface with powdered sugar. Roll kneaded and softened blue rolled fondant thin. Cut a 2" (5.1 cm) circle. Use a 1½" (3.8 cm) circle to emboss the inside of the cut circle to resemble a border for the button. Use tip #6 to cut the button holes.

2. Roll kneaded and softened orange fondant into a long cone shape for the snowman's nose.

### Important

*Cover the cake board at least a day ahead of time to allow the rolled fondant to become firm and avoid imprinting the soft rolled fondant.*

### More to Know

*Add an edible snowlike effect using desiccated (finely cut unsweetened coconut) to party trays, as is shown with these sandwich cookies.*

3. Use a paring knife to cut small grooves in the orange cone to resemble a carrot. Use tip #6 to cut the button holes in the blue button. Roll kneaded and softened red rolled fondant thin. Cut a 1½" (3.8 cm) circle. Use a 1" (2.5 cm) circle to emboss the inside of the cut circle to resemble a border for the button. Use tip #6 to cut the button holes.

4. Bake a 6" (15.2 cm) ball cake and an 8" (20.3 cm) ball cake, following instructions for baking on page 20. Ice the cake with white buttercream, following instructions on page 32. Place the iced cakes on the fondant-covered board. Sprinkle white edible glitter on top of the iced snowman.

5. Add the carrot nose, rolled fondant buttons, and black candy rocks for the mouth. For the eyes, roll two equal size balls using kneaded and softened black rolled fondant. Place the eyes on the snowman.

6. Roll kneaded and softened green fondant thin. Using a mini pizza cutter, cut two rolled fondant strips for the scarf. One strip should be approximately 1¼" × 8" (3.2 × 20.3 cm); the other strip should be 1¼" × 5" (3.2 × 12.7 cm).

**7.** Add fringe to the end of the 5" (12.7 cm) long strip. Arrange the cut strips on the cake for the snowman's scarf.

**8.** Dust the work surface with powdered sugar. Roll kneaded and softened white fondant thin. Using a snowflake plunger cutter, firmly press into the rolled fondant, holding the base of the cutter—do not hold onto the plunger when cutting. The snowflake should remain in the cutter. If the snowflake remains on the work surface and not in the cutter, dust the surface with additional powdered sugar before cutting more snowflakes

**9.** Lift the cutter and gently run your finger along the edge of the cutter to ensure the cut is clean. Place the cutter containing the cut snowflake on the countertop and push the trigger to emboss the snowflake details.

**10.** Lift and push the trigger again to release the cut snowflake. Attach the snowflakes to the cake board using piping gel.

# HOT CHOCOLATE CUPCAKES

**You Will Need**

standard cupcake pan
buttercream icing, white
cinnamon
tip #1M
Styrofoam cups
striped straws

**Techniques**

Baking Cupcakes, page 24
Icing Cupcakes, page 33
Buttercream Basics, page 28

1. Bake and cool chocolate cupcakes, following instructions on page 24. When the cupcakes are cool, remove the cupcake paper.

2. Drop the cupcake into the Styrofoam cup.

3. Fill a pastry bag fitted with star tip #1M with white buttercream icing. Pipe icing on top of the cupcake. Sprinkle the icing with a light dusting of cinnamon. Insert the paper straw.

## Younger Kids

*Little kids will love to peel back cupcake liners and drop the cupcake into the paper cup. When helping with the cake, allow younger kids to sprinkle the edible glitter and arrange the snowman's features.*

# PIPED SNOWMAN AND SNOWFLAKE COOKIES

★★★

**You Will Need**

sandwich cookies

dipping tool

candy coating in blue and white

candy writer in orange, black, and white

**Technique**

Coordinating Party Treats, page 48

1. Dip sandwich cookies in white or blue candy coating, following instructions on page 51. Allow the dipped cookies to set completely.

2. When the candy coating has hardened, pipe details with melted candy from candy writers (page 48).

## Coordinating Treats

*Decorate powdered donuts to create a treat with a snowy feel. Dip cake balls in white chocolate candy coating and then sprinkle them with edible glitter. Or arrange white chocolate snowflake suckers in a bouquet. When making the snowflake suckers, use regular sucker sticks. Slip decorative straws over the sticks before arranging them in the glass container. The glass container is filled ¾ full with candy clay (page 52) leaving 1" (2.5 cm) between the candy clay and the sides of the glass jar. This allows the red Sixlets to conceal the candy clay. The candy clay is used as a filler and to place and arrange the sticks in the pot.*

# About the Author

AUTUMN CARPENTER'S passion for decorating started at a very young age. As a child, she would spend time at the home of her grandmother, Hall of Fame sugar artist Mildred Brand. Later, her mother, Vi Whittington, became the owner of a retail cake and candy supply shop. Her grandmother provided many recipes, while her mother instilled a work ethic, a passion for the art, and served as the best teacher and mentor that Autumn has ever had.

Autumn Carpenter has demonstrated throughout the country and served as a judge in cake decorating competitions. She has been a member, teacher, and demonstrator at the International Cake Exploration Society (ICES) for 20 years.

Autumn is co-owner of Country Kitchen SweetArt, a retail cake and candy supply store that has been owned and operated within Autumn's family for over 45 years. The business caters to walk-in store sales, catalog sales, and an online store, www.shopcountrykitchen.com.

Autumn's own line of useful tools and equipment for cake and cookie decorating can be found online as well as in many cake and candy supply stores throughout the United States and in several other countries. She has written several books, including *The Complete Photo Guide to Cake Decorating* and *The Complete Photo Guide to Cookie Decorating*.

## Resources

*Country Kitchen SweetArt*
A one-stop shop carrying the cake and candy supplies throughout the book.

*Autumn Carpenter Designs*
Mini cookie cutters, perfection strips, texture mats, soccer ball texture set

*Blog*
www.autumncarpenter.wordpress.com

*Websites*
www.autumncarpenter.com
www.cookiedecorating.com
www.shopcountrykitchen.com

# Acknowledgments

SPECIAL THANKS TO Mom, Jenny, and Nancey who let me take over their kitchens for several hours. A big thank you to my mom for helping me on photo-shoot days by keeping things clean and fast paced! Thanks to all the kids who helped decorate the goodies. I had a lot of fun hanging out with all of you. Special thanks to my own kids who helped with many of the projects. Thank you to my husband for his wonderful support. I love you all!

Thanks to Dan Brand, at Brand Photodesign, for fabulous photos and for being so awesome with all those kids.

Thanks to my editor Linda Neubauer and the team at Creative Publishing international for their great support.

# THANKS TO ALL THE KIDS WHO HELPED WITH THE BOOK.

*First row:* Sydney, Austin, Lydia, Jillian, Helen
*Second row:* Cayman, Avery, John Paul, Natalie, Mada
*Third row:* Preston, Paige, Eleanor, Isaac, Landon
*Fourth row:* Annie, Samantha, Simon, Joe, Eden
*Fifth row:* Ryan, Abby, Reena, Annika, Brad
*Sixth row:* Lauren

# Index

# MORE BOOKS ON DECORATING CAKES, CUPCAKES, AND COOKIES!

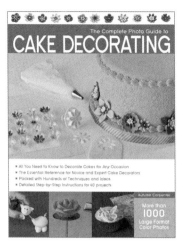

*The Complete Photo Guide to Cake Decorating*

Autumn Carpenter
ISBN: 9781589236691

*The Complete Photo Guide to Cookie Decorating*

Autumn Carpenter
ISBN: 9781589237483

*1,000 Ideas for Decorating Cupcakes, Cookies & Cakes*

Sandra Salamony
and Gina M. Brown
ISBN: 9781592536511

*Cupcake Decorating Lab*

Bridget Thibeault
ISBN: 9781592538317

**Creative Publishing international**

Available online or at your local craft or book store.
www.CreativePub.com

**Our books are available as E-Books, too!**
Many of our bestselling titles are now available as E-Books.
Visit www.Qbookshop.com to find links to e-vendors!